STUDENT SOLUTIONS MANUAL
for
Hildebrand and Ott's
BASIC STATISTICAL IDEAS FOR MANAGERS

David K. Hildebrand
Department of Statistics
Wharton School
University of Pennsylvania

and

Patricia J. Hildebrand
School of Arts and Sciences Computing
University of Pennsylvania

assisted by

Jeffrey D. Hildebrand
Department of Mathematics
University of Wisconsin

Duxbury Press
An Imprint of Wadsworth Publishing Company
I(T)P® An International Thomson Publishing Company

Belmont • Albany • Bonn • Boston • Cincinnati • Detroit • London • Madrid • Melbourne
Mexico City • New York • Paris • San Francisco • Singapore • Tokyo • Toronto • Washington

Wadsworth Publishing Company
10 Davis Drive
Belmont, California 94002, USA

International Thomson Publishing
Europe
Berkshire House 168-173
High Holborn
London, WC1V 7AA, England

Thomas Nelson Australia
102 Dodds Street
South Melbourne 3205
Victoria, Australia

Nelson Canada
1120 Birchmount Road
Scarborough, Ontario
Canada M1K 5G4

International Thomson Editores
Campos Eliseos 385, Piso 7
Col. Polanco
11560 México D.F. México

International Thomson Publishing
GmbH
Königswinterer Strasse 418
53227 Bonn, Germany

International Thomson Publishing Asia
221 Henderson Road
#05-10 Henderson Building
Singapore 0315

International Thomson Publishing Japan
Hirakawacho Kyowa Building, 3F
2-2-1 Hirakawacho
Chiyoda-ku, Tokyo 102, Japan

ISBN 0-534-25526-4

Table of Contents

Solutions to Selected Exercises

Foreword

We have written this Student's Solution Manual to aid students. The manual contains solutions to about one-third of the exercises in the Hildebrand and Ott text. We have tended to include more exercises from the early part of each chapter and relatively fewer from the end-of-chapter exercises, to help students to grow accustomed to the style of the exercises. Keeping in mind that our ideas aren't familiar to everyone, we have tried to be clear and elementary in our reasoning.

We hope that no one will be insulted by too rudimentary a level of presentation. In particular, our solutions to exercises were written to be presented directly to students seeing the material for the first time. Therefore, some of the answers may seem obvious to those who have seen the ideas before.

In preparing this manual, we have worked very hard to avoid errors. However, we may have made misteaks that haven't been caught. If so, please let us know.

We hope that the manual and the text are satisfying.

David K. Hildebrand
Patricia J. Hildebrand

Wynnewood, PA
July, 1995

Chapter 2

Summarizing Data about One Variable

2.1   The Distribution of Values of a Variable

2.1 a. Recall that a histogram is a graphic display of data summarized in a frequency table. Values are arranged along the horizontal axis and counts up the vertical axis. The first step is construct a frequency table for the number of finished cars produced per 8-hour shift. To summarize the data, we must group the values into classes and count how many are in each class.

With 28 observations, choose a small number of classes, such as 8. The range of numbers is from 324 to 390; one convenient choice of classes takes numbers of finished cars produced to the nearest 10. The result of such a grouping of the data is displayed below:

Class	Midpoint	Frequency
320-329	325	1
330-339	335	1
340-349	345	0
350-359	355	1
360-369	365	6
370-379	375	7
380-389	385	11
390-399	395	1

Note that the number and choice of classes for summarizing data are somewhat arbitrary. Therefore, your frequency table and corresponding histogram may be different from the frequency table and corresponding histogram constructed here. For example, you might have chosen to have midpoints of 320, 330, and so on. This choice would be just as good as the one we used.

The histogram of the data as grouped in the frequency table is displayed below. The histogram shows a long "tail" of data to the left. Thus there seems to be an effective maximum value, with the possibility of falling well short of that maximum.

It's plausible that in most shifts the plant works nearly to capacity, but occasionally the plant has difficulties and produces well below capacity. It would be almost impossible to produce above capacity.

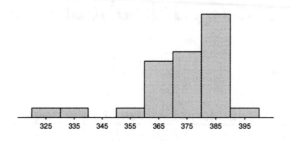

b. Recall that a stem-and-leaf display takes each numerical value, records the leading digit in a "stem" on the left of the display, and the next digit in a "leaf" on the right. In this case, we have to be a bit thoughtful and display the first *two* digits in the stem. Otherwise, we would have only one line, with a stem value of 3, in the display, and we couldn't see anything.

In constructing the stem-and-leaf diagram for these data, the first two digits, 32 through 39, are placed in a column on the left of the diagram. The respective last digits are recorded in the appropriate row on the right of the diagram. The stem-and-leaf of the numbers of finished cars produced is shown below:

```
32 | 4
33 | 9
34 |
35 | 9
36 | 6 0 6 3 7 4
37 | 5 5 9 4 7 1 9
38 | 5 0 4 3 6 7 4 6 5 1 5
39 | 0
```

The stem-and-leaf diagram looks like the histogram turned sideways. (Turn the display a quarter turn.) The display shows a long tail toward low values, which would be on the left in a histogram. Once again, we see left skewness.

2.5 a. A Pareto chart is simply a histogram, with frequencies arranged in order from highest to lowest. Checking the frequencies, we find that Non-Smoking has the highest frequency, 18. Wrong Bed has the second highest frequency, 13. At the right end, there are two categories with the lowest frequency, 1, namely Plumbing and View. When there are ties, we can list the reasons in any order we like; for no reason, we'll put Plumbing before View. As with any histogram, the height of each rectangle is in proportion to the frequency. The labels for the rectangles can be done in several ways. Listing them vertically has the advantage that the labels don't look so "squeezed in."

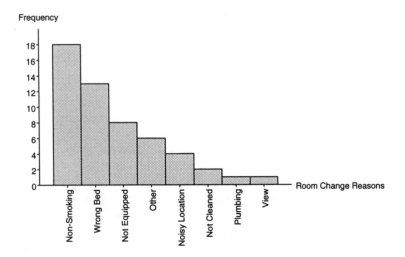

b. The reasons that seem to be related to maintenance and housekeeping are Room not cleaned, Plumbing not working, and perhaps Room not properly equipped. These are *not* the primary reasons shown in the Pareto chart. By far the highest frequencies are Wanted non-smoking room and Wrong type of bed, which are handled in the room registration process. Thus the Pareto chart indicates that registration is the primary problem.

2.2   On the Average: Typical Values

2.6 This is a straightforward exercise in calculation, to make sure you understand the definitions.

For finding the median (and the mode) it is convenient to write the data in order from lowest to highest:

10 10 11 11 12 13 14 14 15 17 17 18 18 18 22 23

There are n = 16 observations, by counting. The mean is just the sum of all the values divided by the number of observations.

$$\bar{y} = (10 + 10 + 11 + \cdots + 23)/16 = 15.1875$$

3

The median is the $(n + 1)/2 = (16 + 1)/2 = 8.5$th score, that is, the average of the 8th and 9th scores. The 8th score is (the second) 14 and the 9th score is 15, so the median is $(14 + 15)/2 = 14.5$. The most frequent value is 18 (3 times), so the mode is 18.

2.3   Measuring Variability

2.11 a. This exercise could be done using a different computer program. The mean and standard deviation may be found from the output to be

$$\bar{y} = 679.38, \qquad\qquad s = 34.83$$

b. Recall that the Empirical Rule says that about 68% of the data should fall within one standard deviation of the mean. This rule works best for well-behaved data, without skewness or outliers.

$$\bar{y} \pm 1s \text{ is } 679.4 - 34.8 = 644.6 \text{ to } 679.4 + 34.8 = 714.2$$

This range includes all but three of the 26 measurements, missing only the 625, 630, and 547 values. So the interval includes $23/26 = .885$ or 88.5% of the data, much more than the 68% indicated by the Empirical Rule. (Presumably, the reason why the rule works badly here is that the 547 outlier makes the standard deviation very big.)

2.12 a. The median was found to be 688 in Exercise 2.8, part b. To find the IQR, we must obtain the 25th and 75th percentiles, as the medians of the bottom and top halves of the data. The 25th percentile of the 26 data values is the median of the smallest 13 values; it is therefore the 7th value, 667. The 75th percentile is the median of the largest 13 values; it is the 7th largest value, 701. The IQR is the difference between these percentiles.

$$IQR = 701 - 667 = 34$$

b. To find the inner fences, the definition says to take the 25th percentile minus 1.5 times the IQR and the 7th percentile plus 1.5 times the IQR. The inner fences are $667 - 1.5(34) = 616$ and $701 + 1.5(34) = 752$. The outer fences use 3 times the IQR rather than 1.5 times, and are $667 - 3(34) = 565$ and $701 + 3(34) = 803$. The 547 value is far below the lower fences (both inner and outer); it is a severe outlier. Note that this outlier inflates the standard deviation so that the Empirical Rule works very badly for these data.

c. The box part of the plot goes from the 25th percentile, 667, to the 75th percentile, 701, with a line indicating the median at 688. The lower whisker part of the plot goes from the smallest non-outlier (625) to the box; the upper whisker goes from the box to the largest non-outlier (the largest value, 711). The outlier value lies beyond the outer fence and therefore is denoted o.

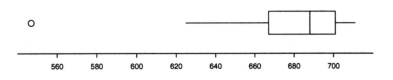

2.22 a. A problem with the mean would show in the top, x-bar chart. The mean chart shows control limits at about 16.67 and 15.33. (These numbers appear on the right side of this particular chart.) The values that are out of control are indicated by a * symbol. There are a large number of * symbols, indicating a serious problem with the mean values. Generally, there is a clear downward trend in the means, as opposed to a sudden drop. It is true that there was a large decrease at day 20, but there is also an evident downward trend elsewhere.

b. Variability should be reflected in the range chart, the second of the control charts. None of the range numbers is even close to the upper control limit, shown on the right of this particular chart as about 2.46. There is no evidence of any kind of problem of excess variability.

2.23 This exercise asks for an interpretation of the results rather than a calculation. The two explanations would lead to different types of out of control patterns. If bad lots were a problem, there ought to be noticeable jumps when a new lot is used. If the problem is with the heating system, there should be more of a drift, rather than a jump, because the change should be gradual. The control chart seems to indicate a decreasing trend in the means, rather than a sudden jump. There doesn't seem to be any identifiable point (except perhaps day 20) at which the means change suddenly. This fact suggests that the problem is a gradual worsening of the heating system.

2.24 a. This exercise calls for computation, to make sure that definitions are understood. The mean is simply the sum divided by the sample size. To compute the sample standard deviation, take deviations from the mean, square them, sum the results, divide by the sample size minus one, and finally take the square root. The following columns of computation facilitate the computation of the sample mean, $\bar{y}$, and standard deviation, s:

y_i	$(y_i - \bar{y})$	$(y_i - \bar{y})^2$
0	-4	16
0	-4	16
0	-4	16
0	-4	16
0	-4	16
0	-4	16
1	-3	9
1	-3	9
1	-3	9
1	-3	9
2	-2	4
2	-2	4
2	-2	4
3	-1	1
3	-1	1
4	0	0
6	2	4
9	5	25
14	10	100
31	27	729

Total	80		1,004

$$\bar{y} = \frac{\sum y_i}{n} = \frac{80}{20} = 4$$

$$s^2 = \frac{\sum(y_i - \bar{y})^2}{n - 1} = \frac{1,004}{19} = 52.84$$

$$s = \sqrt{s^2} = \sqrt{52.84} = 7.27$$

b. Remember that the Empirical Rule says that approximately 68% of the data should fall within one standard deviation of the mean. This rule works best for "nice" data, and should be checked against the actual results. The interval within 1*s* of the mean is 4.00 ± 7.27 or

-3.27 to 11.27

The number of observations that actually fall within this interval is 18 (all except the 14 and the 31), or *90%*. Applying the Empirical Rule, this interval should contain *68%* of the observations which is considerably less than was observed.

The discrepancy is due to the *right-skewness* of the data; 31 is an extreme outlier. The Empirical Rule holds only for a set of measurements having a *mound-shaped* histogram.

2.25 The answer would depend on the computer program used. Most statistical programs have a command to summarize or describe the data. For example, here are results from Minitab, version 10.

```
MTB > name c1 'LveDays'
MTB > set into 'LveDays'
DATA> 0 0 0 0 0 1 1 1 1 2 2 2 3 3 4 6 9 14 31
DATA> end
MTB > describe 'LveDays'

Descriptive Statistics
Variable          N       Mean     Median     TrMean      StDev     SEMean
LveDays          20       4.00       1.50       2.72       7.27       1.63

Variable        Min        Max         Q1         Q3
LveDays        0.00      31.00       0.00       3.75
```

Note that the standard deviation, 7.27, is the same as we calculated by hand using the n - 1 definition. This number agrees with the Excel result except for the amount of roundoff.

2.36 a. This is a very general question, certainly without any "right" answer. One can imagine many sources of variability. One major source of variability would be differences in the representative's ability, training, and effort. Undoubtedly there are other sources, such as weather differences, transportation difficulties, strength of competition, and the like. Your list would no doubt differ from ours.

b. Recall that the "box" of a box plot runs from the 25th to the 75th percentile, with a dividing line at the median. The "whiskers" of a box plot run out to the lowest and highest *nonoutliers*. Skewness is indicated by a lopsided plot, outliers by symbols beyond the whiskers. There doesn't seem to be a great deal of skewness. The box part of the plot is basically symmetric around the median. The two whiskers are just about the same. The plot does indicate several moderate outliers, slightly beyond the ends of the whiskers. Therefore the data seem to be symmetric but heavy-tailed (outlier-prone).

2.37 Recall that a trend is indicated by a generally increasing or generally decreasing pattern as we move from left to right. There may be a slight downward trend. Some, but by no means all, of the highest scores occur toward the left of the plot, and the lowest ones tend to occur a bit more to the right. We wouldn't call it a strong trend at all.

2.38 Yes, this is a silly exercise. Of course, the manager's statement is nonsensical. By definition, half the scores in the data *must* fall below the median. In this case, the mean (average) and median are virtually equal, so half the scores will fall below the mean, also. The manager's finding follows by definition.

2.44 a. To construct a stem and leaf display, we must decide what values go along the left hand, "stem" portion. The natural way to construct a stem-and-leaf display with a width of 10 units (days, in this exercise) is to let the "stem" represent the first digit and the "leaves" the second digit. The data ranges from 10 to 57, so we will need a stem with the digits 1 through 5. Then it's just a matter of recording the second digit of each data point in the leaf. We obtained the following display:

```
1 | 68769692806295487404321912395 7
2 | 96725754555001908107 8
3 | 75
4 | 7905610
5 | 376
```

b. If we want a stem-and-leaf width of 5 days, we'll need to split each "leaf" of 10 in half, with second digits 0, 1, 2, 3, 4 in the first half; 5, 6, 7, 8, and 9 in the second half. The "stem" part of the display will once again range from 1 to 5. Then record the second digit in the leaves. The result (again with unordered "leaves") is as follows:

```
1 | 2024404321123
1 | 68769698695879957
2 | 24001010
2 | 9675755559878
3 |
3 | 75
4 | 010
4 | 7956
5 | 3
5 | 76
```

c. A stem-and-leaf display is a histogram turned sideways, in effect. In both displays, the most obvious pattern is the right-skewed shape of the data. (We can tell it's right skew either by turning the display a quarter turn or by noticing that the long tail goes toward larger values.) Whichever way we choose to display the data, the skewness is clear. A secondary point is the oddity that very few data points are in the range of 30-39 days; this might well be a "bump" in the data of no great importance.

2.45 a. The histogram also shows very substantial right-skewness. There is a long tail to the right of the smoothed histogram.

b. We found right skewness in the stem-and-leaf display. Once again, there is a clear right-skew pattern in the plot of the data. Note the long tail toward the right side of the histogram.
The plots are different because the class intervals are different. The main features of the data are the same.

2.46 Recall that skewness pulls the mean in the direction of the long tail. In this case, the mean is 24, higher than the median, 20. The mean is being pulled up by the right skewness of the data.

2.49 a. Here we want to think, not calculate. The mean is a measure of the middle point of the data, and the value where a histogram would balance. There are many scores in the 20's, 30's and 40's, but a few scores that are much larger, up in the hundreds. The large values will pull up the mean. Therefore, we'd guess that the mean is about 50 or 60.

b. Again, where is the middle of the data? Most BIDPERHR values begin with 0 or 1, but there are some 2 and 3 numbers. Therefore, we'd guess that the mean is about 1.0 or so.

2.50 a. The mean is where each histogram balances. The skewness in the MINPRBID histogram suggests that the mean might be somewhat larger than 50. With such severe skew, it's hard to make a good guess. In the BIDPERHR histogram, the mean seems to be about 1.0, perhaps bigger, but not as large as 2.0.

b. The MINPRBID histogram is severely right-skewed. The BIDPERHR histogram is much less skewed.

2.51 a. No calculations are needed. The respective means are shown as 62.462 and 1.432. Note that we guessed a bit low in previous answers. You may have done better.

b. The reason for the question is that BIDPERHR is defined as 60/MINPRBID. Do the mean values work the same way? No; the value of 60/mean(MINPRBID), 60/62.462, is less than 1.0 and quite different from the mean for BIDPERHR, 1.432. Therefore, the means do not have the same relation as the variables themselves.

2.61 a. Again, you will need to use your particular program to import the data and assign names to the columns. A boxplot from Statgraphics Plus is shown here.

Box-and-Whisker Plot

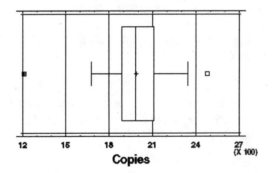

Copies

Note that there are two outliers, a minor one at about 2500 and a major one at about 1200. Otherwise the boxplot is reasonably symmetric.

b. By looking through the data, we find that day 5 has a value close to 2500, namely 2477. Day 25 has a value close to 1200, namely 1207.

c. The mean and standard deviation can be obtained from a data summarization step in virtually every package. The mean of all 44 days is 1985.5, and the standard deviation is 200.8. Your computer package may well round off the answer differently.

d. Delete observations 5 and 25, using whatever editing ability your program has. Using the revised data, the mean and standard deviation can be found in the same way as part c. The mean becomes 1992.3, and the standard deviation becomes 146.9. By deleting the outliers, we have changed the mean very little, but the standard deviation has decreased a great deal.

2.62 a. Here is a plot drawn by StatGraphics Plus. Any other package should give a similar result.

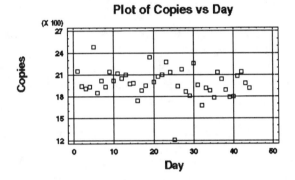

b. There may be a slight downward trend, but certainly not a grossly obvious one. The points seem to be moving downward slightly. The most obvious problem is one point that is far from the rest.

c. We don't see a really strong cyclical component. In particular, there doesn't seem to be a dropoff every seventh day.

Chapter 3

A First Look at Probability

3.1   Basic Principles of Probability

3.10 Again, we are picking one outcome at random. Using the classical interpretation, simply count outcomes.

a. A customer recalling the commercial at all is placed in either the favorable or the unfavorable category.   From the totals,

$$P(favorable) = 95/250 = .38 \qquad P(unfavorable) = 50/250 = .20$$

Therefore,

$$P(recalled) = P(favorable) + P(unfavorable) = .38 + .20 = .58$$

We could also add from the body of the table. Customers recalling the commercial include Men, Favorable (38), Men, Unfavorable (20), Women, Favorable (57), and Women, Unfavorable (30), for a total of 38 + 20 + 57 + 30 = 145. Therefore

$$P(recalled) = 145/250 = .58$$

once again.

b. A customer who does *not* recall the commercial is placed in the incorrect category.

$$P(incorrect) = 105/250 = .42$$

We find the complementary probability by subtraction from 1.

$$P(recalled) = 1 - P(incorrect) = 1 - .42 = .58$$

3.11 Notice that we can't use the basic addition principle, because the events man and favorable are not mutually exclusive. One way to do the calculation is to break up the event into all its mutually exclusive cases.

$$P(\text{man or favorable}) = P(\text{man and incorrect})$$
$$+ P(\text{man and favorable})$$
$$+ P(\text{man and unfavorable})$$
$$+ P(\text{woman and favorable})$$

$$= 42/250 + 38/250 + 20/250 + 57/250$$

$$= 157/250 = .628$$

There are several other ways to do the problem. We could use add the 100 men and the 57 favorable women to get the 157, or, using the general addition principle, subtract the 63 incorrect women and the 30 unfavorable women from 250 to get the 157 again.

3.12 a. The conditional probabilities for men may be found by dividing the response frequencies in the "men" row by the total number of men, 100. For example,

$$P(\text{Incorrect}|\text{Favorable}) = 42/100 = .42$$

For women, divide the frequencies by the total number of women, 150. The results are shown in the next table.

	Incorrect	Favorable	Unfavorable
Men	.42	.38	.20
Women	.42	.38	.20

b. The response probabilities are exactly the same for the two groups. For example, $P(\text{Incorrect}|\text{Men}) = .42 = P(\text{Incorrect}|\text{Women})$. Therefore there are no gender differences at all in the responses.

3.2   Statistical Independence

3.14 We are selecting one outcome (worker) at random. We have the relevant numbers of each type of worker, so we can use the classical interpretation of probability. All we must do is count outcomes.

a. A total of 192 + 248 = 440 workers from 2 plants of the firm were surveyed, 192 from plant 1 and 248 from plant 2. Therefore, the probability that "worker came from plant 1" is

$$P(A) = \frac{192}{440} = .436$$

A total of 48 + 80 = 128 workers responded "poor" to the specified question; 48 from plant 1 and 80 from plant 2. Therefore, the probability of a "poor" response is

$$P(B) = \frac{128}{440} = .291$$

Forty-eight plant 1 workers responded "poor" to the question. Therefore, the probability that "worker comes from plant 1" and "responded poor" is

$$P(A \cap B) = \frac{48}{440} = .109$$

b. The multiplication law for independent events states that if events A and B are independent, then P(A and B) = P(A)P(B).

From part a, we have that P(A and B) = .109, P(A) = .436, and P(B) = .291.

$$P(A)P(B) = .436(.291) = .127$$

Since P(A∩B) ≠ P(A)P(B), events A and B are *not* independent.

Alternatively, we could compute P(B|A) and compare the result to P(B). From part a,

$$P(B|A) = P(A \text{ and } B)/P(A) = .109/.436 = .250$$

This is not the same as P(B) = .291, so once again we have shown that the events are not independent.

c. 48 of the 192 plant 1 workers responded "poor". Therefore

$$P(B|A) = \frac{48}{192} = .25$$

80 of the 248 plant 2 workers responded "poor". Therefore,

$$P(B|\bar{A}) = \frac{80}{248} = .323$$

14

$$P(B|A) \neq P(B|\bar{A})$$

Note that, because A and B are not independent, $P(B|A)$ should not equal $P(B|\bar{A})$; it does not.

3.15 A and B are independent. Therefore,

$$P(B|A) = \frac{P(B)P(A)}{P(A)} = P(B)$$

In order to find $P(B|\bar{A})$, we need to find $P(B$ and $\bar{A})$ since

$$P(B|\bar{A}) = \frac{P(B \cap \bar{A})}{P(\bar{A})}$$

We know that $P(B) = P(A$ and $B) + P(\bar{A}$ and $B)$, because each worker in event B is either in A or in not-A. Therefore,

$$P(\bar{A} \text{ and } B) = P(B) - P(A \text{ and } B)$$

Because A and B are independent, $P(A$ and $B) = P(A)P(B)$. So

$$P(\bar{A} \text{ and } B) = P(B) - P(A)P(B)$$

$$= P(B)[1 - P(A)]$$

$$= P(B)P(\bar{A})$$

This proves that $\bar{A}$ and B are independent. Therefore,

$$P(B|\bar{A}) = \frac{P(B)P(\bar{A})}{P(\bar{A})} = P(B)$$

Because $P(B|A) = P(B)$ and $P(B|\bar{A}) = P(B)$, we have showed that $P(B|A) = P(B|\bar{A})$.

3.18 A good first step in working on most probability problems is to write down the relevant information. The problem states that

P(standard memory) = .84

P(both drives) = .40
P(standard memory and both drives) = .24

a. We can use the definition of conditional probability here.

$$P(\text{both drives}|\text{standard memory}) = \frac{P(\text{both drives and standard memory})}{P(\text{standard memory})}$$

$$= .24/.84 = .286$$

b. Notice that we have reversed which is the random event and which is the given event, as compared to part a. Again, use the definition of conditional probability.

$$P(\text{standard memory}|\text{both drives}) = \frac{P(\text{standard memory and both drives})}{P(\text{both drives})}$$

$$= .24/.40 = .600$$

c. They are not independent. One way to see this is to notice that P(standard memory|both drives) = .60, but P(standard memory) = .84. The occurrence of "both drives" changes the probability of "standard memory" so they can't be independent events. Alternatively,
P(both drives)P(standard memory) = (.40)(.84) = .336, which is not the same as P(both drives and standard memory) = .40.

3.3 Probability Tables, Trees, and Simulations

3.24 A good way to start this (and most) probability problems is to write down what information is given. The exercise states probabilities for the first test.

P(major at first test) = .6
P(minor at first test) = .3
P(none at first test) = .1

The table in the exercise states conditional probabilities of the retest result given the first test result. For example,

P(major at retest|major at first test) = .3

Incidentally, we can tell that the conditional probabilities are for retest given first test, not the other way around. Conditional probabilities must add to 1 for a specified "given." In this exercise, the probabilities add to 1 across each row, but not down each column. Therefore, the row must be the "given."

a. To construct a joint probability table of all first-test, retest possibilities, first put any known marginal probabilities on the appropriate "margins" of the table. In the statement of the problem, we are given first-test marginal probabilities,

$$P(\text{major}) = .60 \qquad P(\text{minor}) = .30 \qquad P(\text{none}) = .10$$

Second, fill in the body of the table using the multiplication law; that is P(A and B) = P(B)P(A|B). Note that for the given conditional probabilities, the conditioning event is first-test errors.

Example:

P(major bugs at retest and major bugs at first-test) =

P(major bugs at 1st-test)·P(major bugs at retest|major bugs at 1st-test)

$$= .60(.30) = .18$$

The complete joint probability table, calculated in the same way, is as follows:

	Retest			
First Test	major	minor	none	
major	.6(.3) = .18	.6(.5) = .30	.6(.2) = .12	.60
minor	.3(.1) = .03	.3(.3) = .09	.3(.6) = .18	.30
none	.1(0) = 0	.1(.2) = .02	.1(.8) = .08	.10
	.21	.41	.38	1.00

b. From the joint probability table in part a,

P(major at retest) = .21

We simply added all the joint probabilities in the "major at retest" column.

c. From the joint probability table in part a, adding in the appropriate column,

P(minor at retest) = .41

and

17

$$P(\text{none at retest}) = .38$$

3.25 To construct a probability tree diagram:

(1) Construct branches for a set of events with known marginal probabilities. In Exercise 3.24, the marginal probabilities for first-test bugs are given.

(2) At the tip of each of these branches, construct branches for another set of events, using *conditional* probabilities. Conditional probabilities are given in Exercise 3.24 with first-test bugs as the conditioning event.

(3) Multiply probabilities along each path to find the probability of each sequence of branches. This will yield the joint probabilities of first-test, retest possibilities.

(4) Add the probabilities of all paths which satisfy a particular event to find the total probability of that particular event. This will yield the marginal probabilities for the retest bugs.

The tree diagram is shown below:

1st test		retest		
		Major	.3	.6(.3) = .18
Major	.60	Minor	.5	.6(.5) = .30
		None	.2	.6(.2) = .12
		Major	.1	.3(.1) = .03
Minor	.30	Minor	.3	.3(.3) = .09
		None	.6	.3(.6) = .18
		Major	0	.1(0) = 0
None	.10	Minor	.2	.1(.2) = .02
		None	.8	.1(.8) = .08

$$P(\text{major at retest}) = .18 + .03 + 0 = .21$$

$$P(\text{minor at retest}) = .30 + .09 + .02 = .41$$

18

$$P(\text{none at retest}) = .12 + .18 + .08 = .38$$

3.26 a. We add a third set of branches to the branches constructed in Exercise 3.25, using the conditional probabilities of bugs at the third test *given* bugs at both first-test and retest. These conditional probabilities are

P(major at third | major at retest and major at first) = .10
P(major at third | major at retest and minor at first) = .10
P(major at third | major at retest and none at first) = .10

P(minor at third | major at retest and major at first) = .20
P(minor at third | major at retest and minor at first) = .20
P(minor at third | major at retest and none at first) = .20

P(major at third | minor at retest and major at first) = 0
P(major at third | minor at retest and minor at first) = 0
P(major at third | minor at retest and none at first) = 0

P(minor at third | minor at retest and major at first) = .10
P(minor at third | minor at retest and minor at first) = .10
P(minor at third | minor at retest and none at first) = .10

It is assumed that programs showing no bugs at retesting need not go through a third round.

Note: branches must be mutually exclusive and exhaustive so that the probabilities branching from any one tip sum to 1. Therefore, if

P(major at third | major at retest and major at first) = .10

and

P(minor at third | major at retest and major at first) = .20

then

P(none at third | major at retest and major at first) = 1 − (.10 + .20) = 1 − .30 = .70

Similarly the other conditional probabilities of none at 3rd test are 1 minus the sum of the conditional probabilities for major at 3rd test and minor at 3rd test with the same given conditions.

The probability tree is shown below.

1st test		retest		3rd test			

				Major	.1	.6(.3)(.1) = .018	1
		Major	.3	Minor	.2	.6(.3)(.2) = .036	2
				None	.7	.6(.3)(.7) = .126	3
				Major	0	.6(.5)(0) = 0	4
Major	.6	Minor	.5	Minor	.1	.6(.5)(.1) = .030	5
				None	.9	.6(.5)(.9) = .270	6
		None	.2			.6(.2) = .120	7
				Major	.1	.3(.1)(.1) = .003	8
		Major	.1	Minor	.2	.3(.1)(.2) = .006	9
				None	.7	.3(.1)(.7) = .021	10
				Major	0	.3(.3)(0) = 0	11
Minor	.3	Minor	.3	Minor	.1	.3(.3)(.1) = .009	12
				None	.9	.3(.3)(.9) = .081	13
		None	.6			.3(.6) = .180	14
				Major	.1	.1(0)(.1) = 0	15
		Major	0	Minor	.2	.1(0)(.2) = 0	16
				None	.7	.1(0)(.7) = 0	17
				Major	0	.1(.2)(0) = 0	18
None	.1	Minor	.2	Minor	.1	.1(.2)(.1) = .002	19
				None	.9	.1(.2)(.9) = .018	20
		None	.8			.1(.8) = .080	21

b. The probability that a program will show major bugs at all three tests can be found at the end of path 1 on the probability tree diagram,

P(major on first and major on retest and major on third) = .018

c. The probability that a program will show major bugs at the third test can be calculated by adding the probabilities of paths 1, 4, 8, 11, 15, and 18.

$$P(\text{major at third}) = .018 + 0 + .003 + 0 + 0 + 0$$

$$= .021$$

This is different from the answer in part b because, first of all, it's the probability of a different event. Now we are looking for the probability of a major bug at the third test, without regard for what happened on the first test and retest. Numerically, the result differs because path 8 also has a non-zero probability, which we added in.

d. The probability that a program will show no bugs at the second or third test can be calculated by adding the probabilities of paths 3, 6, 7, 10, 13, 14, 17, 20, and 21.

$$P(\text{none after 2 or 3}) = .126 + .270 + .120 + .021 + .081$$

$$+ .18 + 0 + .018 + .08$$

$$= .896$$

3.30 a. The important step in constructing the tree is to form mutually exclusive cases at each branch. In this case, each branch should be either C (for contract) or O (for occasional). At each step, we assume $P(C) = .40$. Note that we're assuming that the probability of C doesn't change depending on the result of previous calls. That is, we're assuming that the calls are independent processes. Complete the tree by multiplying the probabilities along each path.

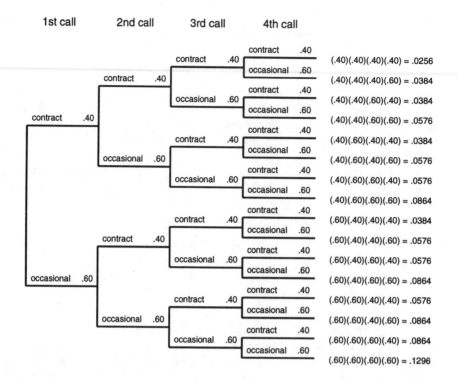

	1st call	2nd call	3rd call	4th call	

1st call   2nd call   3rd call   4th call

contract .40 → contract .40 → contract .40 → contract .40   (.40)(.40)(.40)(.40) = .0256

occasional .60   (.40)(.40)(.40)(.60) = .0384

occasional .60 → contract .40   (.40)(.40)(.60)(.40) = .0384

occasional .60   (.40)(.40)(.60)(.60) = .0576

occasional .60 → contract .40 → contract .40   (.40)(.60)(.40)(.40) = .0384

occasional .60   (.40)(.60)(.40)(.60) = .0576

occasional .60 → contract .40   (.40)(.60)(.60)(.40) = .0576

occasional .60   (.40)(.60)(.60)(.60) = .0864

occasional .60 → contract .40 → contract .40 → contract .40   (.60)(.40)(.40)(.40) = .0384

occasional .60   (.60)(.40)(.40)(.60) = .0576

occasional .60 → contract .40   (.60)(.40)(.60)(.40) = .0576

occasional .60   (.60)(.40)(.60)(.60) = .0864

occasional .60 → contract .40 → contract .40   (.60)(.60)(.40)(.40) = .0576

occasional .60   (.60)(.60)(.40)(.60) = .0864

occasional .60 → contract .40   (.60)(.60)(.60)(.40) = .0864

occasional .60   (.60)(.60)(.60)(.60) = .1296

b. The dispatcher must decline if at least three of the first four calls are from C customers. There are five such paths in the tree, (CCCC), (CCCO), (CCOC), (COCC), and (OCCC). Add their probabilities.

$$P(\text{decline}) = .0256 + .0384 + .0384 + .0384 + .0384 = .1792$$

3.31 Use the definition of conditional probability. Note that P(decline and CCCC) is simply P(CCCC); if the first four customers are C's, the dispatcher will always decline.

$$P(\text{CCCC}|\text{decline}) = \frac{P(\text{decline and CCCC})}{P(\text{decline})} = .0256/.1792 = .143$$

3.34 A typical outcome of this experiment would be one with, say, 18B's, 22C's, and 20D's, indicating that during that month, a random sample of 60 tickets indicated airline A accepted 18 tickets from airline B, 22 tickets from airline C and 20 tickets from airline D.

If we define the outcomes this way, all outcomes should not be regarded as equally likely. The event 60 tickets from B, 0 from C and 0 from D does not necessarily have the same probability of occurring as 20 from B, 20 from C, and 20 from D. For example, if airline B were very large and C and D were small, then the sample would be much more likely to produce a lot of tickets from B since that airline sells more tickets.

3.40 **a.** Suppose that we define event E_1 to be "first selected stock does beat the market." Define E_2 through E_8 similarly. By assumption, the probability of each one of these events is .5. To find the probability that all 8 stocks selected by a securities analyst do indeed beat the market, find the probability

$$P(E_1 \cap E_2 \cap E_3 \cap E_4 \cap E_5 \cap E_6 \cap E_7 \cap E_8)$$

Assuming the random walk theory, this probability is equal to

$$P(E_1)P(E_2)P(E_3)P(E_4)P(E_5)P(E_6)P(E_7)P(E_8)$$

where

$$P(E_i) = .5 \text{ for all i}$$

Therefore,

$$P(\text{all 8 stocks beat the market}) = .5^8 = .00390625$$

b. The two assumptions made in part a are:

(1) independence among stocks--this allowed us to use the multiplication law for independent events in evaluating the 8 event joint probability.

(2) even chance of the stock doing better or worse than the market--this is the reason why it was stated that $P(E_i) = .5$ for all i.

3.41 **a.** In the previous exercise, we found that the chance of getting eight "winners" was .00390625. By complements, the probability of *not* getting eight "winners" is 1 - .00390625 = .99609375.

P(no analyst gets 8 "winners")

    = P(first analyst does not and second does not and ... and 100th does not)

    = P(first does not)P(second does not) ... P(100th does not)

    $= (.99609375)^{100} = .676$

b. Notice that this event is the complement of the event that no analyst gets eight "winners."

    P(at least one analyst gets 8 "winners")

    = 1 − P(no analyst gets 8 "winners")

    $= 1 - (.99609375)^{100}$

    = 1 − .676

    = .324

3.42 a. To construct the table, begin by defining the rows and columns; it doesn't matter which is which. Let's take week 1 as columns, week 2 as rows. To calculate the joint probability table of the various sales levels in week 1 and week 2:

  (1) Put the known marginal probabilities on the appropriate "margins" of the table. In this case, we assume that both sets of marginals are the same.

  (2) Fill in the body of the table using the multiplication law for independent events. In this case, we assume independence of sales from week to week.

The joint probability table is constructed below:

24

	SALES LEVEL				
	Week 1				
Week 2	10	20	30	40	
10	.4(.4) = .16	.3(.4) = .12	.2(.4) = .08	.1(.4) = .04	.40
20	.4(.3) = .12	.3(.3) = .09	.2(.3) = .06	.1(.3) = .03	.30
30	.4(.2) = .08	.3(.2) = .06	.2(.2) = .04	.1(.2) = .02	.20
40	.4(.1) = .04	.3(.1) = .03	.2(.1) = .02	.1(.1) = .01	.10
	.40	.30	.20	.10	1.00

b. Notice that an average sales level of 25 can occur in several ways. We could have sales of 10 in week 1 and 40 in week 2, or 20 and 30, or 30 and 20, or 40 and 10. Therefore,

P(average sales level per week = 25)

= P(sales level of 10 week 1 and sales level of 40 week 2)

+ P(sales level of 20 week 1 and sales level of 30 week 2)

+ P(sales level of 30 week 1 and sales level of 20 week 2)

+ P(sales level of 40 week 1 and sales level of 10 week 2)

= .04 + .06 + .06 + .04, using the table

= .20

3.43 Independence would mean that, for example, a good seller in week 1 is no more (or less) likely to be a good seller in week 2 that a book that sold poorly in week 1. It is doubtful that the independence assumption is at all reasonable. If a recently released book makes the best seller list one week, sales the following week could be greatly affected.

3.49 a. We are given that

P(jacket and trousers) = .22   P(jacket) = .40   P(trousers) = .30

Note that saying that a jacket needs alteration says nothing about whether or not the trousers also need alteration. Start to create a table by defining the rows and columns and inserting the given information.

	Trousers need alteration	Trousers don't need alteration	
Jacket needs alteration	.22		.40
Jacket doesn't need alteration			
	.30		1.00

Then fill in the table by subtraction.

	Trousers need alteration	Trousers don't need alteration	
Jacket needs alteration	.22	.18	.40
Jacket doesn't need alteration	.08	.52	.60
	.30	.70	1.00

P(no alterations) = 1 − (.18 + .22 + .08) = .52

b. In the table constructed in part a, we can find two cases (jacket and not trousers, or trousers and not jacket). We are trying to find the probability of one case or the other, and they are mutually exclusive. Add their probabilities.

P(alterations to jacket or trousers but not both)

$$= P(J \text{ and } \bar{T}) + P(\bar{J} \text{ and } T) = .18 + .08 = .26$$

3.50 There are several ways to check for independence. For example

$$P(J \text{ and } T) = .22$$

but

$$P(J)P(T) = (.40)(.30) = .12$$

Because P(J and T) $\neq$ P(J)P(T), the events aren't independent. Alternatively, we could calculate the conditional probability of T given J and show that it is not equal to the unconditional probability of T.

3.51 **a.** Define J_1 and J_2 to be the events that jacket 1 and jacket 2, respectively, need alteration. The information given indicates that each event should have probability .40. Because we have no additional information, we must assume independence.

$$P(J_1 \cap J_2) = P(J_1)P(J_2) = (.40)(.40) = .16$$

b. We assumed that whether or not one jacket required alteration was independent of whether the other did. We also assumed that the same probability of alteration applied to both. Without any other information the constant-probability assumption isn't unreasonable. But the independence assumption seems dubious. If one jacket did not quite fit, it is more likely that another also would not quite fit. However, you could make a counterargument. The two suits come from different manufacturers and whatever problems arise from the first manufacturer's jackets should have nothing to do with the problems for the second. Not obvious, one way or the other. The best solution would be to gather data!

Review Exercises—Chapters 2 and 3

3.57 a.

Supplier	Mean	Std. dev.	Median	Skew
A	26.71	9.21	23.25	.38
B	31.33	8.49	28.2	.37
C	22.77	9.02	19.8	.33
D	28.05	11.95	24.0	.34

The skew measure used here is (mean - median)/std. dev.

Therefore supplier B appears to have the best (highest) average and the least variability. All of the samples are right skewed, to roughly the same degree. There seem to be serious outliers in the B and D samples, and perhaps in the A sample. These values should be checked for correctness and to see if there was any reason for their unusually good performance.

b. The skewness coefficient indicates that every sample is severely right skewed. As we noted there are several outliers, as well. The Empirical Rule works badly for such data.

3.58 By calculator, the mean is $\bar{y} = 27.215$ and the standard deviation is $s = 9.88$. The variance is $s^2 = (9.88)^2 = 97.56$. The mean could be found as the average of the supplier means. There is no need to weight the means, because the sample sizes are equal. The variance, however, is *not* the average of the supplier variances.

3.71 a. To assess the looks of the data, we need a plot. A stem-and-leaf display for men is shown here.

```
28 | 9
29 |
30 |
31 | 6
32 | 8
33 | 7 1 8
34 | 7 9
35 | 4 1 7 7 2
36 | 8 7 2 5 6
37 | 4
38 | 4
39 | 6
40 | 2
```

The data are nearly symmetric. The mean and median should be nearly equal. The median is the average of the 11th and 12th values, $(35.4 + 35.7)/2 = 35.55$, as shown in the output. The mean is shown as 35.41, very close to the median.

b. The range (largest value minus smallest) for men is 40.2 − 28.9 = 11.3. The range for women is 44.7 − 22.5 = 22.2. The values 44.7 and 22.5 are apparent outliers that inflate the range.

3.72 The boxplot requires calculation of the median, the 25th percentile (median of the bottom half of the data), the 75th percentile (median of the top half), interquartile range, and fences. The lower inner fence is the 25th percentile minus 1.5 times the IQR; the lower outer fence is the 25th percentile minus 3 times the IQR. Similar definitions hold for the upper fences. Sort the data first. The following summary results may be obtained:

	Men	Women
Median	35.55	32.15
25th %ile	33.8	30.5
75th %ile	36.7	33.6
IQR	2.9	3.1
Lower inner fence	29.45	25.85
Upper inner fence	41.05	38.25
Lower outer fence	25.1	21.2
Upper outer fence	45.4	42.9
Outliers	28.9(*)	22.5(*)
		44.7(o)

Draw a box from the 25th to the 75th percentile, with a line at the median. Draw the whiskers to the lowest and highest nonoutliers. Mark the outliers separately.

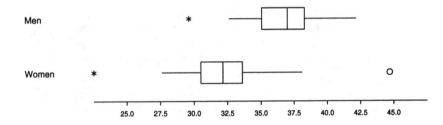

3.73 Because there are 36 values in the combined sample, the median is the average of the 18th and 19th values; median = (33.8 + 34.2)/2 = 34.0. The median has no particular relation to the separate medians. The mean can be found by averaging all 36 or as a weighted average of the means for men and for women, where the weights are the sample sizes:

$$\bar{y} = \frac{20(35.41) + 16(32.41)}{36} = 34.08$$

Chapter 4

Random Variables and Probability Distributions

4.1   Random Variable: Basic Ideas
4.2   Probability Distributions: Discrete Random Variables

4.1 **a.** We could list the first recruiter selected, then the second. Done this way, the possible outcomes for the two persons sampled are

(AB)	(BA)	(CA)	(DA)	(EA)	(FA)	(GA)	(HA)
(AC)	(BC)	(CB)	(DB)	(EB)	(FB)	(GB)	(HB)
(AD)	(BD)	(CD)	(DC)	(EC)	(FC)	(GC)	(HC)
(AE)	(BE)	(CE)	(DE)	(ED)	(FD)	(GD)	(HD)
(AF)	(BF)	(CF)	(DF)	(EF)	(FE)	(GE)	(HE)
(AG)	(BG)	(CG)	(DG)	(EG)	(FG)	(GF)	(HF)
(AH)	(BH)	(CH)	(DH)	(EH)	(FH)	(GH)	(HG)

This sample space consists of 56 outcomes.

Alternatively, we could argue that the order of selection isn't relevant, so that (AB) and (BA) are the same. Done this way, we would have 28 outcomes.

b. Assume that the women are labelled A, B, and C, and the men as D through H. Any random variable assigns a value to each outcome in a sample space. The value of Y, the number of women selected, for each outcome in the sample space is given below (in the order in which the outcomes are listed above):

2	2	2	1	1	1	1	1
2	2	2	1	1	1	1	1
1	1	1	1	1	1	1	1
1	1	1	0	0	0	0	0
1	1	1	0	0	0	0	0
1	1	1	0	0	0	0	0
1	1	1	0	0	0	0	0

4.2 Refer to Exercise 4.1.

The random variable Y takes on the value 0, 1 or 2. Twenty of the 56 possible outcomes in the sample space take on the value 0. Therefore, the probability that Y is 0 is

$$P_Y(0) = \frac{20}{56} = .357$$

Thirty of the 56 outcomes take on the value 1. Therefore, the probability that Y is 1 is

$$P_Y(1) = \frac{30}{56} = .536$$

Six of the 56 outcomes take on the value 2. Therefore, the probability that Y is 2 is

$$P_Y(2) = \frac{6}{56} = .107$$

The probabilities are summarized in the following table

y	0	1	2
$P_Y(y)$	.357	.536	.107

The probability histogram is shown below:

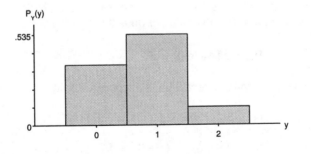

4.3 The cdf of a random variable can be obtained by cumulating (adding) the probabilities, starting with the smallest possible value. Refer to Exercise 4.2, where we calculated the individual probabilities. All we need do is add.

The cdf of Y is shown below:

y	0	1	2
$F_y(y)$	.357	.893	1.00

Below is a plot of $F_y(y)$ against y:

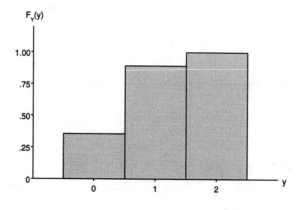

4.3   Expected Value and Standard Deviation

4.15 a. The value $y = 0$ occurs if a controller passes the first test; $y = 1$ and $y = 2$ rework cycles are also possible. No controller goes through more than 2 cycles.

b. $P(Y = 0) = P(\text{pass first test}) = .84$

$P(Y = 1) = P(\text{fail first test})P(\text{pass second}|\text{fail first})$

$= (1 - .84)(.75) = .12$

$P(Y = 2) = 1 - [P(Y = 0) + P(Y = 1)] = 1 - .96 = .04$

4.16 a. The expected value of Y is the probability-weighted average of the possible values 0, 1, and 2. We found the probabilities to be .84, .12, and .04, respectively.

$$E(Y) = 0(.84) + 1(.12) + 2(.04) = .20$$

32

Over the long run of many, many controllers, the average number of rework cycles is .20 per controller.

b. The short-cut formula might save a little arithmetic.

$$\text{Var}(Y) = 0^2(.84) + 1^2(.12) + 2^2(.04) - (.20)^2 = .24$$

$$\sigma_Y = \sqrt{.24} = .4899$$

4.17 a. $P(Y = 0) = P(\text{pass first test}) = .92$

$P(Y = 1) = P(\text{pass second}|\text{fail first})P(\text{fail first})$
          $= .60(.08) = .048$

$P(Y = 2) = 1 - (.920 + .048) = .032$

b. $P(\text{scrapped}) = P(\text{fail first})P(\text{fail second}|\text{fail first})P(\text{fail third}|\text{fail first two})$

For the original data,

$$P(\text{scrapped}) = (.16)(.25)(.10) = .004.$$

For the revised data

$$P(\text{scrapped}) = (.08)(.40)(.20) = .0064, \text{ somewhat higher.}$$

c. $P(Y = 0)$ increases from .84 to .92 under this change, while $P(Y = 1)$ and $P(Y = 2)$ decrease. Because more probability is put on the smallest possible value, the expected value should decrease.

$$E(Y) = 0(.92) + 1(.048) + 2(.032) = .112$$

which is indeed smaller than the original $E(Y) = .20$.

4.4   Joint Probability Distributions and Independence

4.25 a. We want $P(X = 2 \text{ and } Y = 2)$, which is $P_{XY}(2,2)$ by definition

$$P(X = 2 \text{ and } Y = 2) = .100$$

b. There are three cases for which $X = 2 \cap Y \leq 2$. The addition law may be used to find

$$P(X = 2 \cap Y \leq 2) = P(X = 2 \cap Y = 0) + P(X = 2 \cap Y = 1) + P(X = 2 \cap Y = 2)$$

$$= P_{XY}(2,0) + P_{XY}(2,1) + P_{XY}(2,2)$$

$$= .030 + .045 + .100$$

$$= .175$$

c. For this part of the problem, there are nine cases having X and Y both less than or equal to 2. Add probabilities for all cases satisfying the event. So

$$P(X \leq 2 \cap Y \leq 2) = P_{XY}(0,0) + P_{XY}(0,1) + P_{XY}(0,2)$$

$$+ P_{XY}(1,0) + P_{XY}(1,1) + P_{XY}(1,2)$$

$$+ P_{XY}(2,0) + P_{XY}(2,1) + P_{XY}(2,2)$$

$$= .010 + .015 + .030$$

$$+ .020 + .030 + .045$$

$$+ .030 + .045 + .100$$

$$= .325$$

4.26 a. To find $P_X(x)$, sum $P_{XY}(x,y)$ over all y values. For example,

$$P_X(0) = \sum_y P_{XY}(0,y)$$

that is, sum all the probabilities in the $x = 0$ row.

$$P_X(0) = P_{XY}(0,0) + \cdots + P_{XY}(0,4)$$

$$= .010 + .015 + .030 + .075 + .050$$

$$= .180$$

The results are shown here

x	0	1	2	3	4
$P_X(x)$	.180	.195	.250	.195	.180

To find $P_Y(y)$, add probabilities down columns

y	0	1	2	3	4
$P_Y(y)$	.150	.225	.250	.225	.150

b. To test for independence, we must see if $P_{XY}(x,y) = P_X(x)P_Y(y)$ for every x and y. For $x = 0$ and $y = 0$

$$P_{XY}(0,0) = .010 \text{ but } P_X(0)P_Y(0) = (.180)(.150) = .027$$

Therefore X and Y are not independent.

4.27 To calculate $P_{Y|X}(y \mid x) = P_{XY}(x,y)/P_X(x)$ we must divide the joint probabilities by the appropriate marginal probability for the given x value. For example

$$P_{Y|X}(0 \mid 0) = P_{XY}(0,0)/P_X(0) = .010/.180 = 1/18 = .0556$$

The result is conveniently shown by a table

$P_{Y|X}(y \mid x)$

			y		
x	0	1	2	3	4
0	.0556	.0833	.1667	.4167	.2778
1	.1026	.1538	.2308	.3077	.2051
2	.1200	.1800	.4000	.1800	.1200
3	.2051	.3077	.2308	.1538	.1026
4	.2778	.4167	.1667	.0833	.0556

If X and Y were independent, the conditional probabilities for Y would be the same, regardless of the x value. But in this exercise, the conditional probability of any particular y value changes as the x value changes. Thus X and Y are not independent.

4.5 Covariance and Correlation of Random Variables

4.32 a. One way to solve the problem is to set up a tree, with branches for the first block (defective or not, with probabilities .1 and .9) and then the second block (same branches). Alternatively we could use a table.

		Second defective?		
		Y	N	
First defective?	Y	.01	.09	.1
	N	.09	.81	.9
		.1	.9	

Note that $X = 2$ for the (Y,Y) entry of the table, $X = 0$ for the (N,N) entry, and $X = 1$ for the other two entries.

x	0	1	2
$P_x(x)$	.81	.18	.01

b. By definition,

$$\mu_x = \Sigma\, xP_x(x) = 0(.81) + 1(.18) + 2(.01) = .20$$

Informally, we could also argue that we expect .10 defects per block and therefore expect .20 defects in two blocks.

$$\sigma_x^2 = (0 - .20)^2(.81) + (1 - .20)^2(.18) + (2 - .20)^2(.01)$$

$$= .18$$

The shortcut calculation of the variance might also be used.

c. We assumed independence between the two blocks. It might be that the drilling process produces a series of consecutive defects, because of drill wear or

36

misalignment. If so, and if the blocks were selected one right after the other, independence would be an unreasonable assumption.

4.33 For each hole, we can branch on whether or not the drilling is defective. If it is, we branch on whether or not the defect is detected. The rest of the tree follows standard methods. We can find x and y values for each path simply by counting how many defectives and how many detected defects there are along that path.

First		Second				
defective?	detected?	defective?	detected?	x	y	prob
			Y .90	2	2	.0081
		Y .10	N .10			
	Y .90			2	1	.0009
		N .90	N 1.00	1	1	.0810
Y .10			Y .90	2	1	.0009
		Y .10	N .10			
	N .10			2	0	.0001
		N .90	N 1.00	1	0	.0090
			Y .90	1	1	.0810
		Y .10	N .10			
N .90	N 1.00			1	0	.0090
		N .90	N 1.00	0	0	.8100

$P_{XY}(x,y)$

			y		
		0	1	2	
	0	.8100	0	0	.81
x	1	.0180	.1620	0	.18
	2	.0001	.0018	.0081	.01
		.8281	.1638	.0081	

4.34 a. The marginal probability distribution of Y is shown along the bottom margin of the table in Exercise 4.33. By definition

$$\mu_Y = 0(.8281) + 1(.1638) + 2(.0081) = .1800$$

The shortcut method for calculating the variance saves some arithmetic here.

$$\sigma_Y^2 = 0^2(.8281) + 1^2(.1638) + 2^2(.0081) - (.1800)^2$$

$$= .1638$$

$$\sigma_Y = \sqrt{.1638} = .4047$$

b. First, we must find $\text{Cov}(X, Y)$. Again the shortcut method saves a bit of work. Multiply together each pair of values, weight by the joint probability of that pair, sum, and subtract the product of the means.

$$\text{Cov}(X, Y) = \sum_x \sum_y xy P_{XY}(x,y) - \mu_X \mu_Y$$

$$= 0 \cdot 0(.8100) + 0 \cdot 1(0) + 0 \cdot 2(0)$$

$$+ 1 \cdot 0(.0180) + 1 \cdot 1(.1620) + 1 \cdot 2(0)$$

$$+ 2 \cdot 0(.0001) + 2 \cdot 1(.0018) + 2 \cdot 2(.0081)$$

$$- (.20)(.18)$$

$$= .162$$

We have found $\sigma_X = \sqrt{.18}$ and $\sigma_Y = \sqrt{.1638}$

The correlation of X and Y is

$$\rho_{XY} = \frac{\text{Cov}(X, Y)}{\sigma_{XY}} = \frac{.162}{\sqrt{.18}\sqrt{.1638}} = .943$$

c. Recall that X = number of defects present and Y = number of defects detected. Presumably, as the number of actual defects increases, the number of detected defects should also increase. The more defects there are, the more that will be found. Therefore, the correlation should be positive.

4.41 **a.** Obtain the cdf by summing probabilities for values less than or equal to the specified one. $F_Y(y)$ is tabulated below.

y	$F_Y(y)$
0	.21
1	.59
2	.79
3	.90
4	.96
5	.99
6	1.00

b. To find $E(Y)$, use the probability weighted average

$$E(Y) = \sum_{\text{all } y} y P_Y(y)$$

Therefore,

$$E(Y) = 0(.21) + 1(.38) + 2(.20) + 3(.11) + 4(.06) + 5(.03) + 6(.01)$$

$$= 1.56$$

To find σ_Y^2, and thereby σ_Y, we will use

$$\sigma_Y^2 = \sum_{\text{all } y} y^2 P_Y(y) - \mu_Y^2$$

$$= [0^2(.21) + 1^2(.38) + 2^2(.20) + 3^2(.11) + 4^2(.06) + 5^2(.03) + 6^2(.01)] - (1.56)^2$$

$$= 1.8064$$

Therefore,

$$\sigma_Y = \sqrt{1.8064} = 1.34$$

4.42 a. Assuming that the number of customers on successive days are statistically independent, we may use the following independence definition to calculate the joint probability, $P_{Y_1Y_2}(y_1,y_2)$.

$$P_{Y_1Y_2}(y_1,y_2) = P_{Y_1}(y_1)P_{Y_2}(y_2) \quad \text{for } all \ y_1, \ y_2$$

For example $P_{Y_1Y_2}(0,0)=(.21)(.21)=.0441$. The calculated joint probabilities are reported in the joint probability table below:

		0	1	2	3	4	5	6
					Y_2			
	0	.0441	.0798	.0420	.0231	.0126	.0063	.0021
	1	.0798	.1444	.0760	.0418	.0228	.0114	.0038
	2	.0420	.0760	.0400	.0220	.0120	.0060	.0020
Y_1	3	.0231	.0418	.0220	.0121	.0066	.0033	.0011
	4	.0126	.0228	.0120	.0066	.0036	.0018	.0006
	5	.0063	.0114	.0060	.0033	.0018	.0009	.0003
	6	.0021	.0038	.0020	.0011	.0006	.0003	.0001

b. Let $S = Y_1 + Y_2$ be the two-day total number of customers. We need to find the probabilities, $P_S(s)$, associated with each possible s.

From the joint probability table, the desired probabilities can be found by summing the appropriate diagonals

	0	1	2	3	4	5	6
0	$s=0$	$s=1$	$s=2$	$s=3$	$s=4$		
1	$s=1$	$s=2$	$s=3$	$s=4$			
2	$s=2$	$s=3$	$s=4$				
3	$s=3$	$s=4$					
4	$s=4$						
5				etc.			
6							

$P_S(s)$ is given in the table below:

s	$P_S(s)$
0	.0441
1	.1596
2	.2284
3	.1982
4	.1488
5	.1022
6	.0631
7	.0328
8	.0142
9	.0058
10	.0021
11	.0006
12	.0001

c. We could calculate $E(S)$ and $Var(S)$ from the definitions. Alternatively, we may add the expected values of the terms of the sum.

$$E(S) = E(Y_1) + E(Y_2)$$

$$= 1.56 + 1.56$$

$$= 3.12$$

from Exercise 4.65. The variance of a sum of independent random variables is the sum of their separate variances, because the covariance is 0.

$$Var(S) = Var(Y_1) + Var(Y_2) \quad \text{by independence}$$

$$= 1.8064 + 1.8064$$

$$= 3.6128$$

$$\sigma_S = 1.9007$$

This is simply a shorter way to do the calculations. The definitions could certainly be used as well.

Chapter 5

Some Special Probability Distributions

5.1   Counting Possible Outcomes

5.1 In a counting question, the first issue to consider is whether we must take order into account. There is no need to consider the sequence (order) in which the three judges are chosen. Therefore, the combination rule applies.

$$\binom{r}{k} = \frac{r!}{k!(r-k)!}$$

Three judges are chosen from a group of seven judges, that is "7 choose 3", so that $r = 7$ and $k = 3$. Therefore, the number of distinct panels that can be formed is

$$\binom{7}{3} = \frac{7!}{3!4!}$$

5.2 Now we have to choose from two categories, "potentially sympathetic" judges, and the rest. To obtain all panels with exactly 2 "potentially sympathetic" judges, we can combine any of the $\binom{5}{2}$ choices of 2 from the 5 "potentially sympathetic" judges with any of the $\binom{2}{1}$ choices of 1 from the 2 "non-potentially sympathetic" judges. Since any choice of "sympathetic judges" can be matched with any choice of "non-sympathetic" judge, there are $\binom{5}{2}\binom{2}{1} = 20$ panels having exactly 2 "potentially sympathetic" judges.

The number of panels having at least 2 such judges is equal to the *sum* of the number of panels having exactly 2 such judges *plus* the number of panels having exactly 3 such judges; that is

$$\binom{5}{2}\binom{2}{1} + \binom{5}{3}\binom{2}{0} = 30$$

5.9 a. We think so. Each customer is a trial, the probability of taking the discount shouldn't change in any systematic way from customer to customer, and the customers' decisions should be independent. We are counting the number of successes in a specified number of trials.

b. Assuming that binomial probabilities apply, we can use Appendix Table 1 in the text to find the probability that exactly 5 customers of the next 20 take the discount. Find the entry for n = 20, π = .30 and y = 5. The probability is .1789.

c. Now we must add the relevant probabilities. To find P(5 or fewer customers take the discount), use Table 1, identify n = 20, π = .30 and add entries for y = 0, 1, 2, 3, 4, 5 and get .4163.

d. This problem requires a bit of thought. There is no formula given in the text. Look through the entries for n = 20, π = .30 in Appendix Table 1. The most probable number of discount-takers in the next 20 customers is 6, since the entry for n = 20, π = .30 and y = 6 is .1916 which is greater than all other probabilities in that column. As it happens, the expected value (long-run average) value is also 6. In this case the mode (most probable value) just happens to equal the mean (expected value).

5.10 To find the expected value of the number of discount takers, we could use the definition and look up the probabilities for all possible number of discount takers or, as we will do here, use the fact that for binomial probabilities

$$E(Y) = n\pi$$

Therefore,

$$E(Y) = 20(.30) = 6$$

To find the standard deviation of the number of discount takers, we could again use the definition and Table 1 or more simply use the fact that for binomial probabilities

$$\sigma_Y = \sqrt{n\pi(1 - \pi)}$$

Therefore,

$$\sigma_Y = \sqrt{20(.30)(.70)} = 2.05$$

5.11 The interval within 1 standard deviation of the mean is 6 ± 2.05 or 3.95 to 8.05. The possible values are 4, 5, 6, 7, 8. Applying the Empirical Rule, $P(4 \le y \le 8)$ should be about .68. That is, the interval 4 to 8 should contain approximately 68% of the observations.

Using the binomial tables, identify $n = 20$, $\pi = .30$ and add the entries for $y = 4, 5, 6, 7, 8$ and get .7796. The approximation is not terribly good, probably because the distribution has a limited number of possible values and is skewed.

5.3   The Poisson Distribution

5.24 Y is the number of tire failures in a 1,000 mile drive. Y has a Poisson distribution. We need to calculate the mean for 1,000 miles, not 10,000.

$$\mu = \text{(expected number per unit distance)(distance)}$$

$$= \left(\frac{4}{10,000} \right)(1,000) = .4$$

Appendix Table 2 is used to find the following probabilities.

a. $P(Y = 0) = .6703$

b. $P(Y \ge 2) = 1 - P(Y \le 1) = 1 - [P(Y = 0) + P(Y = 1)] = 1 - .9384 = .0616$

5.25 In Exercise 5.24, we found that the mean was .4. For a Poisson distribution, the standard deviation is the square root of the mean.

$$E(Y) = \mu = .4$$

$$\sigma_Y = \sqrt{\mu} = \sqrt{.4} = .632$$

5.4   The Normal Distribution

5.32 The random variable Y is normally distributed with $\mu = 980$ and $\sigma = 40$.

For each of the following problems:

    1) convert the probability statement to its Z score equivalent

    2) draw appropriate pictures

    3) find the probability using Appendix Table 3

a. $P(Y \geq 1{,}000) = P\left(\dfrac{Y-\mu}{\sigma} \geq \dfrac{1{,}000 - 980}{40} \right) = P(Z \geq .5) = .3085$

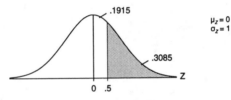

$\mu_Y = 980$
$\sigma_Y = 40$

$\mu_Z = 0$
$\sigma_Z = 1$

.1915

.3085

b. $P(Y \leq 940) = P\left(\dfrac{Y-\mu}{\sigma} \leq \dfrac{940 - 980}{40} \right) = P(Z \leq -1) = .1587$

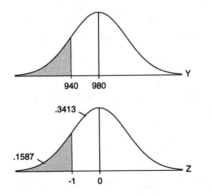

.3413

.1587

c.

$$P(960 \leq Y \leq 1{,}060) = P\left(\frac{960 - 980}{40} \leq \frac{Y - \mu}{\sigma} \leq \frac{1{,}060 - 980}{40} \right)$$

$$= P(-.5 \leq Z \leq 2)$$

$$= .4772 + .1915 = .6687$$

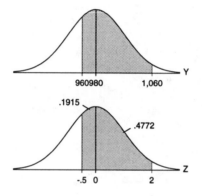

5.33 As in Exercise 5.32, Y is a normally distributed random variable with $\mu = 980$ and $\sigma = 40$.

For each of the following problems:

  1) convert the probability statement to its Z score equivalent

  2) draw pictures of the given probability

  3) specify the z score associated with the given probability using Table 3. This is just the number of standard deviations that Y lies from μ.

  4) solve for k, by equating equivalent quantities

a. $$P(Y \geq k) = P\left(Z \geq \frac{k - 980}{40} \right) = P(Z \geq -z) = .90$$

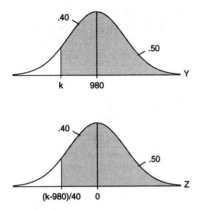

Finding z such that $P(Z \geq -z) = .90$ is equivalent to finding z such that $P(Z \leq z) = .90$. To find $P(Z \leq z) = .90$, specify the area $P(0 \leq Z \leq z)$, which has to be .40. From Table 3, an area of .40 corresponds to $Z = 1.28$. Therefore,

$$P(Z \geq -1.28) = .90$$

Equating equivalent quantities, we have that

$$\frac{k - 980}{40} = -1.28$$

Solving for k, we have that $k = 980 - 1.28(40) = 928.8$

b. $$P(Y > k) = P\left(Z > \frac{k - 980}{40}\right) = P(Z > -z) = .60$$

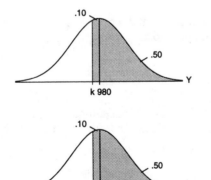

Finding z such that $P(Z > -z) = .60$ is equivalent to finding z such that $P(Z < z) = .60$. To find z such that $P(Z < z) = .60$, specify the area $P(0 < Z < z)$ which has to be .10. From Table 3, an area of .10 corresponds to $z = .25$. Therefore,

$$P(Z > -.25) = .60.$$

Equating equivalent quantities, we have that

$$\frac{k - 980}{40} = -.25$$

Solving for k, we have $k = 980 - .25(40) = 970$.

Supplementary Exercises

5.35 a. Recall the basic properties of a binomial experiment.

1. There are n Bernoulli trials, each one resulting in either S or F.

    In this problem, 100 phone numbers are selected for testing; therefore, $n = 100$. Phone numbers are either residential or business. Therefore, define S to be the outcome that the number belongs to a business phone and define F to be the outcome that the number belongs to a residential phone.

2. The probability of a success, $\pi = P(S)$ remains constant over trials.

    The manufacturer claims that the business phone rate is 15%. The assumption of constant probability seems plausible; the numbers are chosen randomly.

3. The trials are independent.

    There is no reason to doubt this assumption. Phone numbers are randomly selected, and the outcomes from call to call should in no way influence each other.

Yes, the binomial assumptions are met in this situation.

b. We can use Appendix Table 1 to find the probability that at least 24 of the numbers will belong to business phones.

$$P(Y \geq 24) = P(Y = 24) + P(Y = 25) + \cdots + P(Y = 100)$$

Identify n = 100, π = .15 and add entries for y = 24, · · ·, 100 and get .012.

c. Assuming that the claim is true (π = .15), then P(Y ≥ 24) = .012 which is a rather small probability. It would be quite unlikely to get as many as 24 business phones. Therefore, if in fact 24 of the 100 numbers turn out to be business phones, we would doubt the manufacturer's claim.

5.36 We could use Appendix Table 1 to list the probabilities, multiply each value by its probability, and sum. There's an easier way. To find the expected value of Y, the number of business phones, use the result for the binomial distribution that

$$E(Y) = n\pi$$

with *n* = 100 and π = .15

Therefore,

$$E(Y) = 100(.15) = 15$$

To find the variance of Y, use the result for the binomial distribution that

$$\sigma_Y^2 = n\pi(1 - \pi)$$

Therefore,

$$\sigma_Y^2 = 100(.15)(.85) = 12.75$$

5.48 a. As with most counting problems, we must consider whether order matters. Clearly, there's no need to consider order here, so combinations, not permutations, are relevant. To obtain one individual from each division, we have $\binom{5}{1}$ = 5 choices from the first division, $\binom{6}{1}$ = 6 from the second, and $\binom{4}{1}$ = 4 from the third. Thus there are (5)(6)(4) = 120 combinations meeting the conditions.

b. The CEO must choose 3 individuals from a set of 5 + 6 + 4 = 15 individuals. There are

$$\binom{15}{3} = \frac{15!}{3!12!} = 455$$

possible choices. If exactly y are to be chosen from division A (and therefore $3 - y$ are to be chosen from other divisions) there are

$$\binom{5}{y}\binom{10}{3-y}$$

possibilities. To find $P(Y \geq 2)$, add the probabilities for $y = 2$ and 3.

$$P(Y \geq 2) = \frac{\binom{5}{2}\binom{10}{1}}{455} + \frac{\binom{5}{3}\binom{10}{0}}{455} = \frac{110}{455} = .2418$$

5.49 Note that this is not a binomial situation. There is dependence because selection of one person from division A decreases the number available for future choices. Therefore, the binomial formulas don't apply and we need to got back to definitions. We can calculate the probabilities for $y = 0$, 1, 2, or 3 as in the previous exercise. The probabilities are 120/455, 225/455, 100/455, and 10/455, respectively.

$$E(Y) = 0(120/455) + 1(225/455) + 2(100/455) + 3(10/455) = 1.0$$

$$\text{Var}(Y) = 0^2(120/455) + 1^2(225/455) + 2^2(100/455) + 3^2(10/455) - 1^2$$

$$= 0.5714$$

5.58 a. Assuming that requests arrive randomly over time, Y should have a Poisson distribution with mean (1.5/hour)(8 hours) = 12.0. Therefore

$$\mu_Y = 12.0$$

$$\sigma_Y^2 = \mu_Y = 12.0$$

$$\sigma_Y = \sqrt{12.0} = 3.464$$

b. Note that $Y = 8$ is not included in the event. From Appendix Table 2 with $\mu = 12.0$

$$P(Y > 8) = P_Y(9) + P_Y(10) + \cdots = .0874 + .1048 + \cdots = .8450$$

5.59 To say that the time between requests is at least two hours is to say that there are 0 requests in the next two hours. The expected number of requests is 1.5(2) = 3.0. From Appendix Table 2 with $\mu = 3.0$,

$$P(Y = 0) = .0498$$

5.60 a. The assumption of constant expected rate is not critical for Poisson probabilities. The mean number of requests would be

$$\mu_Y = 1(4) + 2(4) = 12.0$$

just as in part a of Exercise 5.58. The probability wouldn't change.

b. This probability would change. The probability would depend on whether the two hours were early or late in the day.

Chapter 6

Random Sampling and Sampling Distributions

6.1   Random Sampling

6.3 a. For true random sampling, all possible combinations of 50 books must have equal probability of being sampled. In this process, books that are shelved far from each other could not be in the same sample. Thus not all combinations would have equal probability; some would have probability 0.

b. Obtain an inventory list of all book titles and number the books. Use a table of random numbers (or computer generated random numbers) to select 50 books to be examined.

6.4 Use a table of four-digit random numbers (or have a computer program generate them). Number the purchasers from 0001 to 4256. If a random number between 0001 and 4256 comes up, sample that purchaser; otherwise go to the next random number. Continue until the desired sample size is obtained.

6.2   Sample Statistics and Sampling Distributions

6.9 a. If a simulation study involves 1,000 independent trials, then the expected value and standard error of the simulation (sample) mean should be

$$E(\bar{Y}) = \mu = 28.2$$

and

$$\sigma_{\bar{Y}} = \frac{\sigma}{\sqrt{n}} = \frac{6.9}{\sqrt{1{,}000}} = .218$$

b. If 4,000 trials are simulated, then the expected value and standard error of the simulation (sample) mean should be

$$E(\bar{Y}) = 28.2$$

and

$$\sigma_{\bar{Y}} = \frac{\sigma}{\sqrt{n}} = \frac{6.9}{\sqrt{4,000}} = .109$$

6.3 Sampling Distributions for Means and Sums

6.12 a. A histogram of the population distribution is shown below:

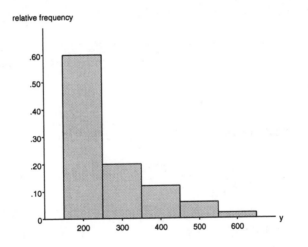

The population distribution is, very obviously, skewed right.

b.

Sample Size n	Interval $\mu_{\bar{Y}} \pm 2\sigma_{\bar{Y}}$	$P(\mu_{\bar{Y}} - 2\sigma_{\bar{Y}} < \bar{Y} < \mu_{\bar{Y}} + 2\sigma_{\bar{Y}})$	Normal Approx.
2	125.08 to 414.92	$1 - (0 + .0336) = .9664$	.95
4	167.54 to 372.46	$1 - (0 + .0521) = .9479$	.95
8	197.54 to 342.46	$1 - (0 + .0319) = .9681$	.95
16	218.76 to 321.24	$1 - (.0173 + .0295) = .9532$	.95
32	233.78 to 306.22	$1 - (.0127 + .0340) = .9533$	.95

As an example of how the table is filled in, we go through the steps for n = 2.

The interval within 2 standard errors of the mean of $\bar{Y}$ is

$$\mu_{\bar{Y}} \pm 2\sigma_{\bar{Y}} = 270 \pm 2(72.46) \text{ or } 125.08 \text{ to } 414.92$$

The exact probability that $\bar{Y}$ falls within this interval can be calculated from the given exact probability calculations.

Note, that $P(\bar{Y} < \mu_{\bar{Y}} - 2\sigma_{\bar{Y}})$ and $P(\bar{Y} > \mu_{\bar{Y}} + 2\sigma_{\bar{Y}})$ are given, whereas we need to calculate $P(\mu_{\bar{Y}} - 2\sigma_{\bar{Y}} < \bar{Y} < \mu_{\bar{Y}} + 2\sigma_{\bar{Y}})$. In order to find the desired probability, note that

$$P(\mu_{\bar{Y}} \, 2\sigma_{\bar{Y}} < \bar{Y} < \mu_{\bar{Y}} + 2\sigma_{\bar{Y}}) = 1 - [P(\bar{Y} < \mu_{\bar{Y}} - 2\sigma_{\bar{Y}}) + P(\bar{Y} > \mu_{\bar{Y}} + 2\sigma_{\bar{Y}})]$$

so that

$$P(125.08 < \bar{Y} < 414.92) = 1 - (0 + .0336)$$

$$= 1 - .0336$$

$$= .9664$$

The approximation is fairly close, and improves slightly as *n* increases.

c. Part b is repeated for $\bar{Y}$ within 1 standard error of $\mu_{\bar{Y}}$

Sample Size n	Interval $\mu_{\bar{Y}} \pm \sigma_{\bar{Y}}$	$P(\mu_{\bar{Y}} - \sigma_{\bar{Y}} < \bar{Y} < \mu_{\bar{Y}} + \sigma_{\bar{Y}})$	Normal Approx.
2	194.54 to 342.46	$1 - (0 + .2160) = .7840$	.68
4	218.77 to 321.23	$1 - (.1296 + .1965) = .6739$	.68
8	233.77 to 306.23	$1 - (.1460 + .1594) = .6946$	.68
16	244.38 to 295.62	$1 - (.1876 + .1486) = .6638$	.68
32	251.89 to 288.11	$1 - (.1543 + .1473) = .6984$	.68

The approximation is quite good except when *n* = 2.

6.13 a. Because of the Central Limit Theorem, for a random sample of 50 new claims, the sampling distribution of $\bar{Y}$ is approximately normal with

$$\mu_{\bar{Y}} = \mu = 927$$

$$\sigma_{\bar{Y}} = \frac{\sigma}{\sqrt{n}} = \frac{871}{\sqrt{50}} = 123.2$$

b. $P(\bar{Y} > 1,100) = P\left(\dfrac{\bar{Y} - \mu_{\bar{Y}}}{\sigma_{\bar{Y}}} > \dfrac{1,100 - 927}{123.2} \right) = P(Z > 1.40)$

$$= .0808$$

6.18 a. We are dealing with an individual value, not a mean, so there is no reason to consider the standard error of the sample mean. Again, we could think of this problem as dealing with a "mean of a sample of 1."

$P(.997 < Y < 1.003) = P((.997 - 1.000)/.006 < Z < (1.003 - 1.000)/.006)$

$$= P(-.50 < Z < .50)$$

The area for $z = .50$ is found in Appendix Table 3 as .1915. Because we want the area between $z = -.50$ and $z = .50$, we must add the areas between $-.50$ and 0 and between 0 and .50. The two areas are both .1915 by the symmetry of the normal curve. Therefore the desired probability is $.1915 + .1915 = 2(.1915) = .3830$.

b. Now we are concerned with the mean of a sample of 20 pins. The relevant standard error is $\sigma/\sqrt{n} = .006/\sqrt{20} = .0013$. Therefore

$P(.997 < \bar{Y} < 1.003) = P((.997 - 1.000)/.0013 < Z < (1.003 - 1.000)/.0013)$

$$= P(-2.24 < Z < 2.24)$$

The table area for $z = 2.24$ is .4875. Again we are concerned about a probability from $-z$ to z, so the desired probability is $2(.4875) = .9750$.

c. If the variability increases, the probability of a high-quality connection should go down. There will be fewer pins with the right diameter and more that are too large or too small.

$$P(.997 < Y < 1.003) = P((.997 - 1.000)/.020 < Z < (1.003 - 1.000)/.020)$$

$$= P(-.15 < Z < .15) = 2(.0596) = .1192$$

This probability is, indeed, lower than the one found in part (a).

d. The standard error of the sample mean becomes $.020/\sqrt{20} = .0045$. So

$$P(.997 < \bar{Y} < 1.003) = P((0.997 - 1.000)/.0045 < Z < (1.003 - 1.000)/.0045)$$

$$= P(-.67 < Z < .67) = 2(.2486) = .4972$$

This is lower than the answer in part b, because of the greater variability.

6.19 The description of the distribution of pin diameters indicates that the distribution is outlier-prone (heavy-tailed). There is nothing in the description that suggests any skewness in one direction or the other. For a symmetric, but outlier-prone, population distribution, the Central Limit Theorem works well even for samples of size 20. Therefore, the answer to part (b) of the previous exercise is most likely very close to correct. Note, though, that the answer to part (a), about a single observation, could be seriously incorrect if the population distribution is outlier-prone.

6.4   Checking Normality

6.25 In such a simulation, the average value is an approximation to the expected value, the long run average, of the statistic. The result indicates that the expected value of the sample median is very nearly 0. The standard deviation of a statistic is a simulation approximation to its standard error. The standard error of the sample median is just about .2.

6.26 When a normal plot looks like a straight line, the distribution is close to normal. A straight line is a straight line, regardless of which axis is which.

6.31 a. The testing itself is basically destructive. Testing would wear the door lock mechanism so that it couldn't be sold as new. For any destructive testing, sampling is absolutely essential, or there won't be anything left to sell.

b. If the supplier knew or suspected that such a sampling mechanism were used, it would be easy to place five (or a few more) high-quality mechanisms at the head of the batch, thus guaranteeing that the batch would pass inspection, even if the lot were bad.

6.32 This question requires some thought, not a formula. There are several problems with sampling a fixed percentage of the total. First, it's the absolute sample size that determines the probable accuracy of the sample mean, as indicated by the square root of the sample size in the denominator of the standard error of the mean. The sample fraction is far less relevant. Second, it seems clear that an unknown supplier should be sampled more rigorously. Therefore, the sample size for the new supplier should be larger. Third, sampling half of one percent would yield sample sizes ranging from 5, for the new supplier of door handles, to 250, for the established supplier of trim parts. A sample size of 5 is quite likely to be too small, while a sample of 250 may well be wastefully large.

6.39 a. The demand for a 5-pound sack of flour by an individual customer may be thought of as independent from every other customer. The weekly demand is the sum of these individual demands, and there are most likely a large number of customers for a supermarket. Therefore, by the CLT, the weekly demand of 5-pound sacks of flour can be expected to be roughly normally distributed.

b. One way to select a random sample of size n = 15 would be to visit the store on a randomly selected day of the week at a randomly selected time of the day and observe the number of sacks of flour bought by the first 15 customers to go through the checkout lines. To avoid bias, one would have to be careful about selecting times at random, rather than selecting specific times (such as only when a sale price was not in effect).

6.40 a. For a sample of size n = 15,

$$\mu_{\bar{Y}} = \mu_Y = 72$$

and

$$\sigma_{\bar{Y}} = \frac{\sigma_Y}{\sqrt{n}} = \frac{1.6}{\sqrt{15}} = .413$$

$$P(\bar{Y} > 73.0) = P\left(\frac{\bar{Y} - \mu_{\bar{Y}}}{\sigma_{\bar{Y}}} > \frac{73 - 72}{.413}\right)$$

$$= P(Z > 2.42) = .0078$$

b.

$$P(72 - k \le Y \le 72 + k) = P\left(\frac{72 - k - 72}{.413} \le \frac{\bar{Y} - \mu_{\bar{Y}}}{\sigma_{\bar{Y}}} \le \frac{72 + k - 72}{.413}\right)$$

$$= P\left(\frac{-k}{.413} \le Z \le \frac{k}{.413}\right) = P(-z \le Z \le z) = .95$$

From Table 3, we have that $P(-1.96 \le Z \le 1.96) = .95$. Equating like quantities, we have that

$$z = \frac{k}{.413} = 1.96$$

Solving for k, we have

$$k = 1.96(.413) = .8095$$

Therefore a 95% range for Y is

$$71.1905 \le Y \le 72.8095$$

6.41 a. We can obtain a listing of all of the 2,571 sales categories from the store's accounting system. We could sample every 25th sales category on the list (assuming that the categories are in random order) or have a computer package draw 100 random numbers in the range from 1 to 2,571 and select those sales category codes.

b. A simple random sample may not be desirable. It's possible that there will not be equal representation from the various departments in the department store.

One possible sampling method alternative is to group the 2,571 sales categories into various departments and randomly choose an equal number from within each department to make up your sample.

It may also be known that the largest inventory shrinkage comes from certain sales areas such as clothing or sporting goods. Therefore it may be more desirable to monitor these areas rather than having many small and insignificant sales areas in the sample. Simple random sampling is most likely not the best way to study the problem.

6.42 a. We can use the basic expressions given in the text for the expected value and standard error of a sample mean. The expected value and standard error of the sample average shrinkage for a random sample of 100 categories is

$$E(Y) = \mu = 2.2$$

$$\sigma_{\bar{Y}} = \frac{1.6}{\sqrt{100}} = .16$$

b. As far as the expressions in the book goes, it makes no difference. The expressions for the expected value and standard error are not affected by this distinction.

Technically, the calculations in part a assume sampling with replacement. If the finite population correction factor is used (sampling without replacement), the expected value is the same as in part a, but the standard error changes.

$$E(Y) = \mu = 2.2$$

$$\sigma_{\bar{Y}} = \frac{\sigma}{\sqrt{n}}\sqrt{\frac{N-n}{N-1}} = \frac{1.6}{\sqrt{100}}\sqrt{\frac{2.571-100}{2,571-1}}$$

$$= \frac{1.6}{\sqrt{100}}(.98)$$

$$= .1568$$

The standard errors are very close in value. It doesn't make much difference in part a whether we use without replacement or with replacement sampling. The only time that the finite population correction factor makes any difference, numerically, is in a situation where the sample size is a large fraction of the population size. In this exercise, the sample size is only $100/2,571 \approx 4\%$ of the population size.

6.43 We need to refer to the guidelines for using the Central Limit Theorem. With a sample size of 100, we would expect the normal approximation to be fairly good. A plot of the sample data would indicate to us how much faith we would have in the approximation. If a histogram of the sample data shows obvious and very extreme skewness (and hence suggests extreme skewness for the population distribution), a normal approximation should be used somewhat skeptically. There is no particular reason to expect such extreme skewness here.

Review Exercises—Chapters 4–6

6.51 **a.** Here each change is a trial that can result in a success (error) or failure (correct change). We take Y = number of incorrectly posted changes as a binomial random variable with $n = 50$ and $\pi = .05$. Therefore, we have

$$P(Y \leq 3) = p_Y(0) + p_Y(1) + p_Y(2) + p_Y(3) = \sum_{y=0}^{3} \binom{50}{y} (.05)^y (.95)^{50-y}$$

b. To find a numberical value, we could either have a computer package calculate binomial probabilities, or use a table. We looked in Appendix Table 1 with $n = 50$, in the $\pi = .05$ column. The entries for $y = 0, 1, 2,$ and 3 are .0769, .2025, .2611, and .2199, respectively. The desired probability is the sum of these entries, .7604.

c. We made the binomial assumptions. Certainly, the experiment is a series of success/failure trials. Further Y = the number of successes in a fixed number (50) of trials, and the order of successes and failures is irrelevant. The other assumptions are constant probability of success and independence. Given that sampling is random, it's hard to imagine why the probability of incorrect posting should change over products. The only potentially dubious assumption is independence; one incorrect posting might indicate a badly-trained employee, a turbulent period at the store, or some other reason why other prices might also be more likely to be posted incorrectly. Such reasoning seems somewhat farfetched. Further, a truly random sample should guarantee independence. Therefore, we would expect that the assumptions hold rather well.

6.55 Perhaps one might want to think that each foot of wire is a trial, with a probability .0002 of a success; this reasoning would lead to binomial probabilities. However, why should we make one foot a trial? Why not two feet, or one inch? Instead, we assume that impurities occur randomly over the length of the wire, so that Poisson probabilities will apply. The expected rate is .0002 impurities per foot. The length, 1,000 feet, plays the role of time here. Thus $\mu_Y = (.0002)(1,000) = .2$. The desired probability is

$$p_Y(0) = e^{-0.2}\frac{(0.2)^0}{0!} = .8187$$

The probability may also be found in Appendix Table 2, in the $\mu = .2$ column with $y = 0$.

6.56 In assuming that Poisson probabilities applied, we implicitly made the Poisson assumptions of nonclumping and independence. Thus we assumed that impurities do not occur in bunches at essentially the same place along the wire. Also we assumed that the occurrence of an impurity at one point along the wire does not signal an increased (or decreased) probability of other impurities farther along the wire.

6.59 **a.** To begin answering this question, notice that the information says that there is a 5% chance that any one item is defective. Each item can be considered as a trial. We assume that binomial probabilities apply, with a "success" being a defective item. The information indicates that $n = 20$ and $\pi = .05$. If Y is the number of defectives, $P(Y \geq 2)$ may be found by adding the probabilities in Table 1 for $y = 2, 3, \cdots, 20$.

$$P(Y \geq 2) = .1887 + .0596 + \cdots + .0000 = .2641$$

Alternatively

$$P(Y \geq 2) = 1 - [P_Y(0) + P_Y(1)] = 1 - (.3585 + .3774) = .2641$$

b. We made the binomial assumptions that each item either was or wasn't defective, that the probability of a defective is constant at .05, that the occurrence of a defective doesn't signal an increased (or decreased) probability that another item will be defective, and that the sample size of 20 was fixed.

6.60 No; the sample size can't be regarded as fixed. Instead, there is a continuing sampling. Alternatively we note that because the process considers only the most recent 10 items, the order of successes and failures is relevant.

6.61 It is specified that $\mu = 250$, $\sigma = 70$, and $n = 40$. We want to find the probability that the sample mean $\bar{Y}$ is larger than 265. Nothing has been said about the shape of the underlying distribution. To proceed, we assume that the distribution of $\bar{Y}$ is normal. The mean is $\mu_{\bar{Y}} = \mu = 250$ and the standard error (standard deviation) is

$70/\sqrt{40} = 6.3246$.
Therefore

$$P(\bar{Y} > 265) = P\left(Z > \frac{265 - 250}{70/\sqrt{40}} \right)$$

$$= P(Z > 1.36) = .5 - .4131 = .0869$$

6.62 The key assumption is that the Central Limit Theorem applies, so that the sampling distribution of $\bar{Y}$ would be normal, to a good approximation. If the distribution of individual values is highly skewed, a sample size of 40 might not be adequate to "deskew" the sampling distribution, particularly because the computed probability is a one-tail probability. (We wouldn't get the benefit of a compensating error with one tail too large and the other too small.)

Chapter 7

Point and Interval Estimation

7.1   Point Estimators

7.6 a. All three box plots appear to be symmetric around 0. It appears that all three estimators have expected value (very close to) 0, equal to the population mean. All three seem to be (very close to) unbiased. This makes sense, because the Laplace population is symmetric.

b. The box plot for the median appears to be the narrowest one, by a slight margin as compared to the trimmed mean, and by more compared to the mean. Thus the median appears to be the most efficient of the three methods in this case.

7.7 The averages all are essentially 0, indicating that all three estimators are unbiased. The standard deviation of the sample median is smallest, indicating that the median is most efficient. These were exactly our conclusions in the previous exercise.

7.2   Interval Estimation of a Mean, Known Standard Deviation

7.17 a. The confidence interval is shown in the output under the heading 95.0 PERCENT C.I., as $12.424 \le \mu \le 13.784$. The 95% confidence refers to the fact that, in the long run over many, many samples, 95% of such confidence intervals will include the true population mean value.

b. The confidence interval includes 12.500 as one reasonable value for μ. (It goes as low as 12.424.) Therefore this interval does *not* necessarily indicate that the shop mean differs from 12.5.

7.18 This interval does *not* include 12.500 and therefore indicates that the true, population mean differs from the standard 12.50. This interval carries only 90% confidence and is narrower than the 95% interval in the previous question. The 12.5 value is slightly outside this interval and barely within the previous interval.

7.19 a. The boxplot indicates that the data are right skewed. The right "whisker" is clearly longer than the left one. Actually, the right half of the box may be slightly longer than the left half, as well. In addition, the mild outliers (indicated by the * symbol) are out in the right tail.

b. The Central Limit Theorem applies to probabilities for the sample mean. The sample size is moderate; $n = 48$. The population appears to be skewed, but not terribly much so. According to our guidelines for the CLT, a sample size of 40 or so works reasonably well to assure normality of the sampling distribution of the mean. The claimed 90% confidence may be slightly in error, but shouldn't be terribly wrong.

7.3   Confidence Intervals for a Proportion

7.20 The sample proportion of calls that resulted in new product placements is $\hat{\pi} = 229/500 = .458$.

A general 95% confidence interval for π is

$$\hat{\pi} - z_{\frac{\alpha}{2}}\sqrt{\frac{\hat{\pi}(1 - \hat{\pi})}{n}} \leq \pi \leq \hat{\pi} + z_{\frac{\alpha}{2}}\sqrt{\frac{\hat{\pi}(1 - \hat{\pi})}{n}}$$

where in this case

$$\alpha = .05; \qquad z_{\frac{\alpha}{2}} = z_{.025} = 1.96.$$

Therefore

$$.458 - 1.96\sqrt{\frac{.458(.542)}{500}} \leq \pi \leq .458 + 1.96\sqrt{\frac{.458(.542)}{500}}$$

$$.458 - .0437 \leq \pi \leq .458 + .0437$$

$$.4143 \leq \pi \leq .5017$$

Rounding:

$$.41 \leq \pi \leq .50$$

with 95% confidence

7.21 We are 95% confident that the true long run proportion of new product placements is in the interval (.414,.502). By 95% confident we mean that if this experiment is conducted again and again and a confidence interval calculated for each, we expect 95% of them to include the true long run proportion.

7.4 How Large a Sample is Needed?

7.27 The overage amount per claim for auto body repair is to be estimated. The guess for a value of σ is 400. To determine n, we need the allowable $\pm$ E, the table value, and the standard deviation.

Desired: 95% confidence interval with width of $50, so that

$$2E = 50 \qquad E = 25 \qquad \alpha = .05 \qquad z_{\frac{\alpha}{2}} = 1.96$$

Therefore,

$$n = \frac{(1.96)^2(400)^2}{(25)^2} \approx 983$$

7.28 a. Suppose that the standard deviation is somewhere between 300 and 450; $300 < \sigma < 450$.

If $\sigma = 300$, the required sample size would be

$$n = \frac{(1.96)^2(300)^2}{(25)^2} \approx 553$$

If $\sigma = 450$, the required sample size would be

$$n = \frac{(1.96)^2(450)^2}{(25)^2} \approx 1,245$$

b. If the sample size corresponding to σ = 450 is used (n = 1,245) and σ is really 300, the confidence interval is

$$\bar{y} \pm 1.96 \frac{300}{\sqrt{1,245}}$$

$$\bar{y} \pm 16.66$$

The interval width is only about 33, much smaller than the allowable width of 50.

7.29 Yes. The sample size (983) is much larger than any of our guideline values for application of the Central Limit Theorem in assuming normality of $\bar{Y}$.

7.5   The *t* Distribution

7.31 This is a *t* statistic, because the sample standard deviation is used. The *t* table, Appendix Table 4, with n − 1 = 3 df is used to find the following probabilities. One could also use a computer package that calculates cumulative *t* probabilities.

a.   The value 1.638 is shown in the area = .10 column, which means that P(*t* > 1.638) = .10.

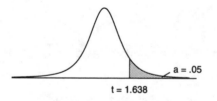

b.   P(*t* > 5.841) = .005

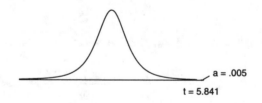

c. $P(t < -2.353) = .05$

$$= P(t > +2.353)$$

because the *t*-distribution is symmetric

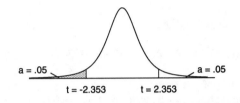

a = .05   a = .05

t = -2.353   t = 2.353

d. The table indicates that there is an area of .05 under the curve to the right of 2.353. By symmetry, there is also are area of .05 under the curve to the left of -2.353. So $P(-2.353 < t < 2.353) = 1 - .05 - .05 = .90$

a = .9

t = -2.353   t = 2.353

e. $P(|t| > 3.182) = P(t < -3.182) + P(t > 3.182)$

$$= .025 + .025 = .05$$

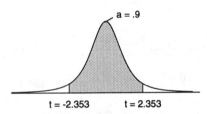

a = .025   a = .025

t = -3.182   t = 3.182

f. $P(|t| > 4.541) = P(t < -4.541) + P(t > 4.541)$

$$= .01 + .01 = .02$$

a = .01   a = .01

t = -4.541   t = 4.541

7.32 $P(t > 1.638) = .10$, with df=3 (if we correctly use the t table)

If we incorrectly use the normal table, $P(Z > 1.638) \approx P(Z > 1.64) = .5 - .4495 = .0505$

$P(|t| > 1.638) = 2P(t > 1.638) = 2(.10) = .20$ df=3 (correctly using the t table)

Erroneous use of normal table: $P(|Z| > 1.638) \approx P(Z > 1.64) = 2(.0505) = .1010$

The mistaken assumption of a normal distribution causes an understatement of the probabilities. Remember that the t-distribution has thicker tails (more probability is contained in the tails) than the z-distribution.

7.6   Confidence Intervals for the t Distribution

7.36 The interval is shown under the heading 95.0 PERCENT C.I. as

$$319.70 \leq \mu \leq 337.59$$

7.37 We don't see any evidence of serious nonnormality. The stem-and-leaf display is not particularly skewed, and there are no outliers.

Supplementary Exercises

7.43 Assume that the sample size will be large enough that the distinction between t and z table values will be irrelevant. For 95% confidence, the z table value (Appendix Table 3) is $z_{.025} = 1.96$. We assume $\sigma = 10,000$ and the problem specifies E = 500. We must solve

$$1.96 \left(\frac{10,000}{\sqrt{n}} \right) = 500$$

to get $\sqrt{n}$ = 1.96(10,000)/500 = 39.2 or n = 1,537. For this *n*, the distinction between *t* tables and *z* tables would be utterly negligible, so the calculation is valid.

7.44 Nonsense! The Central Limit Theorem effect for *n* = 1,537 would guarantee an excellent normal approximation. The objection is silly.

7.53 **a.** When the long-run process standard deviation, σ, is known, the interval can be based on the *z* distribution. This interval is shown as the 90.0 PERCENT C.I. in the output for "zinterval." Note that in this part of the output, Minitab states an assumed sigma; in the "tinterval" portion, it makes no such statement. The interval is

$$16.48 \le \mu \le 20.14$$

b. When we drop the assumption that σ is known, we must use the sample standard deviation, shown as 6.29 in the output. Now we use the "tinterval" part of the output. This interval is shown as the 90.0 PERCENT C.I. in the output for tinterval.

$$16.32 \le \mu \le 20.30$$

c. To see why the intervals differ, look at how the calculations differ. There are only two differences between a *z* interval and a *t* interval—the table value used and the standard deviation used. There are two reasons for the wider interval. The *t* table value, 1.701, is larger than the *z* table value, 1.645, and the sample standard deviation s = 6.29, happened to come out larger than the assumed process standard deviation σ = 6.0.

7.54 In the histogram, the peak is at the left, with a long tail to the right. The data clearly are not normal. They are right skewed.

7.65 **a.** Again, the standard deviation must be based on the sample data, so we need to use the *t* table. For a sample size of 12, there are 11 d.f.; the required *t* table value for tail area .05/2 is 2.201. The confidence interval is

$$117.667 - 2.201\ (20.646)/\sqrt{12} \le \mu \le 117.667 + 2.201\ (20.646)/\sqrt{12}$$

or

$$104.55 \le \mu \le 130.78$$

We could have saved a little arithmetic by noticing that the output gives a standard error of 5.960. We could use this figure instead of calculating $(20.646)/\sqrt{12}$.

b. The value $\mu = 105.2$ is included within the interval, so it is possible that the mean did not change. However, it is also possible that the mean increased to about 130, a very substantial gain. From a sample of size 12, with a great deal of variability in the data, we can't get a very accurate estimate of the change in mean.

7.66 a. In this exercise, we are dealing with a proportion (of boards that aren't salable) rather than a mean. We can use the large-sample z approximation to obtain a confidence interval for the population proportion π. The sample proportion is $\hat{\pi} = 18/144 = .125$. The required z table value for 95% confidence in 1.96. We use $\hat{\pi}$ in place of π in the standard error calculation. The confidence interval is

$$.125 - 1.96\sqrt{(.125)(1 - .125)/144} \le \pi \le .125 + 1.96\sqrt{(.125)(1 - .125)/144}$$

or

$$.071 \le \pi \le .179$$

b. Look at the numerical limits of the interval. The confidence interval doesn't include any values higher than .20. Therefore, there is no reason for concern that the true proportion π is larger than .20.

7.67 a. If the confidence interval is to have a width of .04, the $\pm$ value should be $E = .02$. The required table value is $z_{\frac{\alpha}{2}} = 1.96$. The worst case will occur when $\hat{\pi}$ is as close to .50 as seems reasonable; in this case, that's when $\hat{\pi} = .20$. The required sample size is

$$n = (1.96)^2(.20)(1 - .20)/(.02)^2 = 1536.64, \text{ rounded up to } 1537$$

b. If the true proportion of unsalable boards is .50 (that is, fully half the boards can't be sold), the supplier is not reputable at all. In this situation the worst-case assumption is so disastrous as to be pointless.

7.68 a. Not all boards have an equal probability of being sampled, unless the supplier happened to load the boards in completely random order. Only the boards in the right rear pallet can possibly be sampled. If an unethical supplier knew this fact, it would be easy to put good boards in the right rear and poor boards everywhere else.

b. A completely random sample, taking boards from all over the truckload, might well be so inconvenient as to be infeasible. No doubt, one could dream up all sorts of fancy methods to obtain the sample. The key to any good method is that it should be unpredictable. It shouldn't be possible to know in advance which boards will be sampled. For example, it might be possible to sample a pallet at random from the truck.

7.74 a. Compute the ± term for a confidence interval for a proportion, using a z table value of 1.96, and a sample proportion of .50. The ± term should be
$$1.96\sqrt{(.50)(1-.50)/1500} = .0253.$$

b. The ± term would change to $1.96\sqrt{(.40)(1-.40)/1500} = .0248$. The change is extremely small.

c. A confidence interval only allows for probable random error; it does not account for biases. The additional allowance is presumably for small biases that remain, no matter how carefully the sample is chosen.

7.75 If 30 of 1,500 likely voters favor a candidate, the sample proportion is $\hat{\pi} = 30/1500 = .02$. The desired ± term is $1.96\sqrt{(.02)(1-.02)/1500} = .0071$. This is substantially smaller than .03.

7.81 a. You should obtain a mean of 227.3 and a standard deviation of 79.7, possibly to a different number of digits. Here, for example, is Minitab output.

```
MTB > Describe 'Elapsed'.

Descriptive Statistics


Variable        N      Mean   Median   TrMean    StDev   SEMean
Elapsed        61     227.3    241.0    230.4     79.7     10.2
```

b. A t confidence interval from Minitab is the following. A different package may yield different numbers of decimals.

```
MTB > TInterval 90.0 'Elapsed'.

Variable    N      Mean   StDev  SE Mean       90.0 % C.I.
Elapsed    61     227.3    79.7     10.2  (   210.3,    244.4)
```

7.82 a. A normal plot generated by Minitab is shown below. The choice of which axis is which isn't standard, so with a different package, you might get either choice of axes. A plot from a different graphics package may be slightly different, but the general pattern should be similar. Remember that normally distributed data should show as a straight line. This plot appears to be roughly a line. There is no obvious curve or S shape.

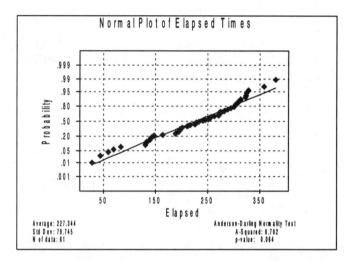

b. The appearance of the plot will depend heavily on which package you use and how you print it out. Here, for example, is a Minitab plot of elapsed time against call number.

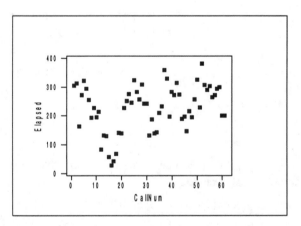

There are clear cycles, with high values following other high values, and lows usually following other lows. This makes sense; in busy periods, all waiting times will tend to be long. In calmer periods, all waits will be short. The presence of cycles indicates a carryover effect from one measurement to the next. This fact is a violation of the assumption of independence.

Chapter 8

Hypothesis Testing

8.1   A Test for a Mean, Known Standard Deviation
8.2   Type II Error, β Probability, and Power of a Test

8.5 We must decide whether to use a one-sided or two-sided research hypothesis. Then we need to formulate a test statistic, and find the rejection region corresponding to the given α. Finally we should actually compute the test statistic and reach a conclusion.

The following is the z test of H_0: $\mu = 1.5$:

H_0: $\mu = 1.5$

H_a: $\mu \neq 1.5$ (Test should be two-sided since we are concerned with both too many and too few unpaid public-service commercials).

T.S.: $z = \dfrac{\bar{y} - \mu_0}{\left(\dfrac{1.6}{\sqrt{18}}\right)} = \dfrac{\bar{y} - 1.5}{\left(\dfrac{1.6}{\sqrt{18}}\right)}$

R.R.:   At the $\alpha = .05$ level, reject H_0 if $z > 1.96$ or $z < -1.96$ (two-tailed test)

Conclusion: $\bar{y} = 1.278$

$$z = \dfrac{1.278 - 1.5}{\left(\dfrac{1.6}{\sqrt{18}}\right)} = -.5887$$

which does not lie in the rejection region. Therefore, do not reject H_0.

8.6 We can calculate β in two ways. Either use the shortcut method in the text, or write the rejection region in terms of the sample mean and calculate a normal probability. Here we will use the longer method; you can check the answers using the shortcut.

If H_0 is rejected whenever

$$z = \frac{\bar{y} - 1.5}{\left(\dfrac{1.6}{\sqrt{18}}\right)} > 1.96 \quad \text{or} \quad z = \frac{\bar{y} - 1.5}{\left(\dfrac{1.6}{\sqrt{18}}\right)} < -1.96$$

then it will be rejected whenever

$$\bar{y} > 1.5 + 1.96\left(\frac{1.6}{\sqrt{18}}\right) = 2.2392 \quad \text{or} \quad \bar{y} < 1.5 - 1.96\left(\frac{1.6}{\sqrt{18}}\right) = .7608$$

Therefore,

$$\beta = P(H_0 \text{ not rejected} \mid \mu_a \text{ true}) = P(.7608 < \bar{y} < 2.2392)$$

$$= P\left(\frac{.7608 - \mu_a}{\left(\dfrac{1.6}{\sqrt{18}}\right)} < z < \frac{2.2392 - \mu_a}{\left(\dfrac{1.6}{\sqrt{18}}\right)}\right)$$

β probabilities for the specified values of μ are calculated using this relation:

μ_a	β
1.0	$P(-.6343 < z < 3.2859) = .7365$
1.2	$P(-1.1646 < z < 2.7556) = .8750$
1.4	$P(-1.6949 < z < 2.2253) = .9419$
1.6	$P(-2.2253 < z < 1.6949) = .9419$
1.8	$P(-2.7556 < z < 1.1646) = .8750$
2.0	$P(-3.2859 < z < .6343) = .7365$

Below is a sketch of the β curve:

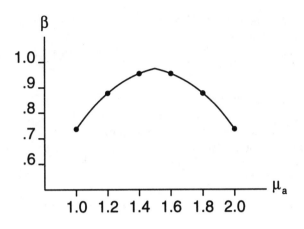

8.7 Below is a histogram-like plot of the data:

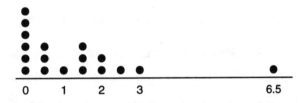

Since n is small (18) and the data are clearly skewed, the assumption of normality of the $\bar{Y}$ distribution is not appropriate. The Central Limit Theorem probably will not work too well for such skewness and such a small n.

8.3   The *p*-Value for a Hypothesis Test

8.8 **a.** We need only look at the output. The value of the *z* statistic is labeled z (which seems reasonable enough) on the computer output; $z = 1.14$.

b. The *p*-value is labelled P VALUE (also reasonably enough) on the computer output; *p*-value = .26.

c. A two-tailed *p*-value is appropriate. The company is concerned with *any* deviation from the goal of 40%. If the proportion is less than .4, the company fears loss of sales. If it is greater than .4, the company fears higher expense accounts.

8.9 a. The *p*-value of .2549 exceeds the usual α values of .1, .05, and .01; therefore the sales manager is correct in concluding that the test was not statistically significant. (Remember the Universal R.R.: Reject H_0 if the *p*-value ≤ the specified α.)

b. According to the results of the test, the probability of obtaining a sample mean of at least 47.6 or at most 40.4 if the true mean is 44 is .2549. The result isn't conclusive, so we don't have enough evidence to support H_a. However, the term "proved" is much too strong a statement; instead, we should say something such as "we haven't enough evidence." With such a small amount of data, we haven't "proved" anything.

8.4   Hypothesis Testing with the *t* Distribution

8.14 Let *d* represent change in gasoline mileage after installation of a certain device.

A sample of 7 cars yielded a mean change of .50 ($\bar{d}$ = .50) and standard deviation of 3.77 (s_d = 3.77).

a. The claim is that the device increases gas mileage. Therefore we want a one-sided research hypothesis. The natural null hypothesis is that the device does nothing; if so, the mean difference over the whole population of cars will be 0. The appropriate null and research hypotheses are

H_0: μ = 0

H_a: μ > 0

b. The "ttest" part of the output shows `Pr > |t| = 0.7378`. This is a two-tailed *p*-value, as indicated by the absolute value sign. To convert to one-tailed, divide by 2 and get a *p*-value of .3689. This is much larger than α = .05, so the data do not strongly support the claim.

8.15 The confidence interval is shown at the end of the output, in the "ci" portion, as

−2.270553 ≤ μ ≤ 3.270553

Rounding:

−2.3 ≤ μ ≤ 3.3 with 90% confidence

If the null hypothesis is true, $\mu = 0$. Because $\mu = 0$ is contained in this interval, we cannot reject the null hypothesis H_0: $\mu = 0$. This agrees with the result of Exercise 8.14.

8.16 No, the agency has not "conclusively established" that the device has *no* effect on mpg. The results indicate that no change in mpg is a possibility but then so are the possible changes of, for example, 3.0 mpg or -1.5 mpg (according to the C.I. of Exercise 8.15). The confidence interval is quite wide, so the β risk for practically relevant μ values will be large and it is unwise to conclude "no change."

8.5 Assumptions for *t* Tests
8.6 Testing a Proportion: Normal Approximation

8.24 a. One way to answer this question is to look at the confidence interval in the output. It shows a 95% confidence interval as

$$.1296 \leq \pi \leq .2645$$

This interval doesn't include the intended value, $\pi = .10$. So it seems reasonable to reject that value as a null hypothesis.

Alternatively, we can compute a z statistic.

$$z = \frac{\hat{\pi} - \pi_0}{\sqrt{(\hat{\pi})(1 - \hat{\pi})/n}}$$

$$= \frac{.1970 - .10}{\sqrt{(.1970)(1 - .1970)/137}} = 2.85$$

This value is larger than the critical value for $\alpha = .05$, 1.96. Once again, we reject the null hypothesis. There is a statistically detectable (significant) deviation from the target .10 value.

b. The two-tailed p-value is the probability of exceeding our actual z statistic, 2.84, in absolute value. (The absolute value is needed for a two-tailed value.) The entry for $z = 2.84$ in Appendix Table 3 is .4977, so the tail area is $.5 - .4977 = .0023$. The two-tailed p-value is twice that, .0046.

8.25 The result from one store in the affected area has a carryover to other stores. That is, if one store had an unusually high demand, we could predict that other stores in the same area would also show unusually high demand. This carryover effect is a violation of the assumption of independence. You might also argue that this is a bias, a systematic overrepresentation of demand. We don't like calling it a bias, because it occurred as a random result and wasn't really systematic.

8.7   Hypothesis Tests and Confidence Intervals

8.28 a. Recall that the confidence interval is calculated as the estimate (sample mean, here) plus-or-minus a table value times a standard error. The required table value is $z_{\alpha/2} = z_{.025} = 1.96$. The standard error is the standard deviation, 1.60, divided by the square root of the sample size, 18. The confidence interval is

$$1.278 - 1.96\,(1.60)/\sqrt{18} \le \mu \le 1.278 + 1.96\,(1.60)/\sqrt{18}$$

or

$$.539 \le \mu \le 2.017$$

b. The 95% confidence level corresponds to $\alpha = .05$. The confidence interval includes the null hypothesis value 1.50, which therefore must be retained. That is the same conclusion we reached previously.

8.29 a. The confidence interval is the standard z interval. The table value is given, the mean is 47.6, the standard deviation is assumed to be 10.0, and the sample size is 10.

$$47.6 - 1.28\,(10.0)/\sqrt{10} \le \mu \le 47.6 + 1.28\,(10.0)/\sqrt{10}$$

or

$$43.55 \le \mu \le 51.65$$

b. The null hypothesis value, $\mu = 44.0$, falls within the 80% confidence interval, so that it must be retained at the corresponding $\alpha = .20$.

c. The value $\mu = 44.0$ is just barely within the interval, falling almost down to the lower end. Thus retaining the value is a "close call."

8.42 a. The standard z (for n = 2,417, it doesn't matter whether we use z or t) confidence interval for the population mean rating, μ, is

$$\bar{y} - z_{\frac{\alpha}{2}} \times \frac{s}{\sqrt{n}} \le \mu \le \bar{y} + z_{\frac{\alpha}{2}} \times \frac{s}{\sqrt{n}}$$

where

$$\alpha = .05; \qquad z_{\alpha/2} = z_{.025} = 1.96$$

Therefore,

$$3.05 - 1.96 \times \frac{.62}{\sqrt{2,417}} \le \mu \le 3.05 + 1.96 \times \frac{.62}{\sqrt{2,417}}$$

$$3.05 - .0247 \le \mu \le 3.05 + .0247$$

$$3.0253 \le \mu \le 3.0747$$

Rounding

$$3.03 \le \mu \le 3.07 \text{ with 95\% confidence.}$$

b. Because we just computed a 95% (a = .05) confidence interval, we might just as well use it to carry out a test.

H_0: $\mu = 3.00$

H_a: $\mu \ne 3.00$

Conclusion: Since 3.00 does not lie in the 95% confidence interval for μ, this null hypothesis can be rejected at the .05 level.

8.43 a. Yes the results were statistically significant. The sample mean was too far away from the stated average value, 3.00, for one to believe that it was due to random fluctuation alone (although there is a very small chance that it was).

b. Yes, this is misleading. In ordinary language, the word "significant" suggests "large" or "important." The statistical use of the word is different, meaning "detectable." The statement without any numerical clarification might tend to give the impression that business executives are completely without conscience, when in fact the deviation from "average" is so small (a small fraction of one point on the scale) that people would most probably ignore it.

8.44 We rejected the null hypothesis using $\alpha = .05$, because the null hypothesis value was not included in the confidence interval. Therefore, we know—using the Universal Rejection Region—that the p-value is less than .05. To get a more accurate handle on its value, we need to carry out a formal test. We are using a two-sided research hypothesis, so we want a two-tailed p-value.

$$p\text{-value} = 2P(Z \geq |z_{actual}|)$$

The actual z test statistic for H_0: $\mu = 3$ is

$$\text{T.S.: } z = \frac{\bar{y} - \mu}{\left(\frac{s}{\sqrt{n}}\right)} = \frac{3.05 - 3}{\left(\frac{.62}{\sqrt{2,417}}\right)} = 3.96$$

Therefore,

$$p\text{-value} = 2P(Z > 3.96) \approx 2P(Z > 4.00) = .00006$$

This indicates that the results are most definitely of statistical significance, although they are not of much practical significance.

8.55 The data aren't too badly skewed, but show some severe outliers. Thus, the data appear heavy-tailed (outlier-prone) rather than normally distributed.

8.56 Note that the data are along the horizontal axis. The data don't seem to fall near the line. Instead, there seems to be something of an S shape, indicating outlier-proneness.

8.57 **a.** We take as the null hypothesis the assertion that the population mean has not changed; H_0: $\mu = 30.4$. The value 30.4 does not fall in the 90% confidence interval, shown as $27.809 \leq \mu \leq 29.987$. Thus, at $\alpha = .10$, we reject the null hypothesis. An α value of .10 is rather large, so the test is not as conclusive as it would be with a smaller α. However, the null hypothesis mean is far enough away from the confidence interval that the result seems conclusive.

b. The most evident nonnormality of the data is outlier-proneness, as opposed to skewness. For $n = 44$, the Central Limit Theorem will work well in such a case. The claimed probabilities should be very good approximations. The outliers make the sample mean an inefficient estimator; that's a different problem. It means that the confidence interval is valid, but may be wider than an interval based on a different method.

8.58 a. The output shows the *t* statistic as -2.32, so all we have to do is compare that to the appropriate table value. We don't have 43 degrees of freedom in the *t* table. The value for area .10/2 = .05 must be something between 1.684 (40 df) and 1.671 (60 df). The actual *t* statistic is shown as -2.32. The absolute value of the *t* statistic is well beyond the tabled values. We can reject H_0.

b. Because the H_0 mean was not in the 90% confidence interval, we also rejected it previously. Our answer in part a was simply a different way of reaching the same conclusion.

c. The *p*-value is shown as 0.025 in the output. Because this value is less than α = .10, once again we reject H_0. Thus, the formal test, the confidence interval, and the *p*-value all lead to the same conclusion, as they must.

8.59 The output shows a *t* statistic equal to -2.34 and a two-tailed *p*-value of .020. We probably should use a one-sided research hypothesis here; the key concern is the possibility of completing processing in less than 96% of all days. Thus we should take a one-tailed *p*-value, which is .010. If we take a "reasonable α level" to be α = .05, the departure from the 96% target is statistically significant. If we use α = .01, the result is right on the edge of being statistically significant. All in all, we appear to have fairly strong evidence of a real (not merely random) departure from the target value.

8.60 If the failures occurred in streaks, the assumption of independence is quite likely violated. If we had independence, the failures should occur randomly. If the independence assumption is violated, the effective sample size is not as large as it appears. Significance results are overstated. We don't have quite as good evidence as we thought that the departure is more than random.

8.61 a. Execustat yielded the following results. Your package may give a different number of decimal places or a different format.

```
Sample size = 49
Mean = 2076.22
Variance = 63000.6
Std. deviation = 250.999
```

```
95% confidence intervals
     Mean:  (2004.13,2148.32)
     Variance:  (43810.2,98357.1)
     Std. deviation:  (209.309,313.619)
```

b. The following results were obtained by entering the "Analyze" section of Execustat, selecting "one sample" from the menu, asking to test a mean, and entering the H_0 mean, 2,299, and requesting the "less than" alternative. The p-value is shown as 0 to four decimal places.

```
                    Hypothesis Test - Mean

Null hypothesis: mean = 2299
Alternative: less than

Computed t statistic = -6.21288
               P value = 0.0000
```

8.62 a. A stem-and-leaf display from Execustat is shown here. Other packages may have results that differ in some details, but the general pattern should be similar.

```
           Stem-and-leaf display for milesreq: unit = 10  1|2 represents
120

            1     15|7
            2     16|6
            7     17|23567
           15     18|04455689
           20     19|33456
          (5)     20|36778
           24     21|0233345678
           14     22|366
           11     23|000238
            5     24|1
            4     25|256
            1     26|0
```

There doesn't seem to be any serious skewness, nor any outliers. The data appear to be normally distributed.

b. A plot of miles against day number obtained from Execustat is shown here. Most programs should give similar graphs.

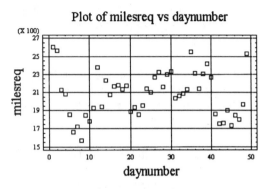

Plot of milesreq vs daynumber

There doesn't seem to be an obvious upward or downward trend, but there does seem to be a cyclic pattern of high days followed by low days. Notice that the values at the beginning of the time series are all high. Then there is a string of low values, then several high values, and so on. There may well be dependence. The test may, therefore, be too conclusive.

Review Exercises—Chapters 7–8

8.74 We have H_a: $\pi < .45$ so we take H_0: $\pi = .45$. (We may ignore the non-boundary values $\pi > .45$ in H_0.) The test statistic is $\hat{\pi}$ = the proportion of buyers out of the next 100 walk-in customers. We convert this proportion to a z statistic.

$$z = \frac{\hat{\pi} - .45}{\sqrt{(.45)(1 - .45)/100}}$$

The (one-sided) rejection region corresponding to $\alpha = .05$ is $z < -1.645$, using the now-familiar value from Appendix Table 3.

8.75 The only change in the test that occurs when we change α is the critical number from the tables. For $\alpha = .01$ (one-tailed), the value from the z table is -2.33.

8.76 The result is $\hat{\pi} = 32$. Therefore

$$z = \frac{.32 - .45}{\sqrt{(.45)(1 - .45)/100}} = -2.61$$

This value is more negative than -1.645 (corresponding to $\alpha = .05$). Therefore we have evidence to support the research hypothesis.

8.77 The z statistic, -2.61, is less than (more negative than) the $\alpha = .0$ cutoff of -2.33. Again we reject H_0. By the Universal Rejection Region (reject H_0 if and only if p-value $< \alpha$) we must have p-value $< \alpha = .01$.

8.89 The confidence interval is shown in the output as

$$78.91 \leq \mu \leq 81.84$$

8.90 The null hypothesis value $\mu = 82.0$ is not included in the 90% confidence interval. Therefore we reject this null hypothesis value at $\alpha = .10$. By the Universal Rejection Region, the p-value must be less than .10.

Chapter 9

Comparing Two Samples

9.1   Comparing the Means of Two Populations

9.5 a. The sample means are labeled MEAN on the computer output:

$$\bar{y}_1 = 10.37 \text{ and } \bar{y}_2 = 9.83$$

The sample standard deviations are labeled S.D. (not S.E., for standard error)

$$s_1 = .3233 \text{ and } s_2 = .2406$$

b. The t statistic value is labeled T and is identified as EQUAL variance:

$$t = 4.24$$

c. The t' statistic value is labeled T and is identified as UNEQUAL variance:

$$t' = 4.24$$

d. The two statistics, t and t' are equal in this case because the sample sizes, n_1 and n_2 are equal.

$$\text{When } n_1 = n_2, \; s_p \sqrt{\frac{1}{n_1} + \frac{1}{n_2}} = \sqrt{\frac{s_1^2}{n_1} + \frac{s_2^2}{n_2}} \text{ so } t = t'$$

e. The assumption of normal populations does not appear seriously violated. And because the variability in the two samples seems similar, and $s_1^2 \approx s_2^2$ (not grossly unequal) and $n_1 = n_2$, the assumption of equal variances is reasonable. There is no reason to think that bias or dependence are problems. There don't seem to be any serious violations of assumptions.

f. The p-value for the pooled variance t test is labelled P. It isn't completely clear whether it is one-tailed or two-tailed. However, there is nothing in the output to indicate which direction a one-sided research hypothesis might have. Furthermore, virtually all computer packages use a general research hypothesis unless something else is stated explicitly. Therefore, we can safely assume that the *p*-value is two-tailed.

$$p\text{-value} = .0005$$

g. Since the *p*-values of both *t* tests are *very* small, the null hypothesis of no decrease in mean potency is rejected at all reasonable levels of α. The data gives strong support to the alternative hypothesis that the mean potencies of the two samples are not equal. The test indicates a *decrease* in mean potency. Notice that this conclusion isn't surprising. The primary question should probably be how much the potency decreases, rather than whether it decreases at all.

9.2   A Nonparametric Test: The Wilcoxon Rank Sum Test

9.10 a. The rank sums are labeled exactly as that on the computer printout:

sample 1 rank sum = 146 and sample 2 rank sum = 64

b. The value of the *z* statistic is located under the heading NORMAL APPROXIMATION WITH CONTINUITY CORRECTION

$$z = 3.062$$

Note: There are slight variations in how various programs calculate this statistic, so a different package may give a slightly different answer.

c. In Exercise 9.5, sample 1 was potency measures of current production, and sample 2 referred to year-old drugs. If there is any effect, current drugs should be more potent than ones that had been sitting around. Therefore, the histogram for currently produced drugs should be concentrated on higher values, on the right of the histogram. If there is no effect of age, the two histograms should be the same except for random variation. The null hypothesis of no age effect says that the two population histograms look the same.

H_0:   Populations are identical

H_a: Population 1 is shifted to the right of population 2.

d. We could look up the calculated *z* statistic in Appendix Table 3.

R.R.:   Reject H_0 if $z > 2.326$ for $\alpha = .01$

Conclusion: Reject H_0. Yes, the research hypothesis is supported at the .01 level.

9.11 a. The output shows the p-value = .0022. This is presumably a two-tailed p-value, because the output does not indicate a direction. A one-tail p-value should be reported, because we have a one-sided research hypothesis. We note that the rank sums do go in the anticipated direction, with sample 1 scores higher than sample 2 scores.

$$p\text{-value} = (.0022)/2 = .0011$$

b. The conclusion of the rank sum test is rejection of the null hypothesis of same location for potency distributions. In English, the data indicate that the drug very clearly loses potency when stored for one year. The conclusions for the rank sum test and the t test agree.

9.3   Paired-Sample Methods
9.4   The Signed Rank Method

9.21 The t statistic value is labelled T on the computer printout: T = -1.806. The p-value is shown as PROB = 0.079. This p-value is greater than $\alpha = .01$, so we cannot claim a statistically detectable difference at that α (or at $\alpha = .05$).

9.22 The normal plot has a very pronounced S shape. This shape indicates that the data are more or less symmetric, but contain outliers. For this reason, the data don't appear to be normal.

9.23 a. The output for the sign test shows a p-value of .003 (under the heading TWO-SIDED PROBABILITIES FOR EACH PAIR OF VARIABLES). This p-value is less than .01, so we should reject the null hypothesis.

b. The p-value is shown under the heading TWO-SIDED PROBABILITIES USING NORMAL APPROXIMATION as .007. This value is also less than $\alpha = .01$, so this test also rejects H_0.

c. Both the sign test and the signed rank test are much more conclusive in rejecting H_0 than is the t test. The reason is the outliers in the data. The t test is less effective in finding a difference (has lower power) in this situation, because the outliers increase the standard deviation and therefore the standard error. The t

statistic is reduced because of this fact. The sign and signed rank tests do not use the actual magnitudes of the numbers, so they are much less affected by outliers.

9.5   Two-Sample Procedures for Proportions

9.24 The 90% confidence interval for the true difference in proportion of bad debts is

$$\hat{\pi}_1 - \hat{\pi}_2 - z_{\alpha/2}\,\sigma_{\hat{\pi}_1-\hat{\pi}_2} \le \pi_1 - \pi_2 \le \hat{\pi}_1 - \hat{\pi}_2 + z_{\alpha/2}\,\sigma_{\hat{\pi}_1-\hat{\pi}_2}$$

where

$$\alpha = .10 \text{ so that } z_{\alpha/2} = 1.645$$

$$\hat{\pi}_1 = \frac{102}{2,128} = .0479 \qquad\qquad \hat{\pi}_2 = \frac{31}{1,072} = .0289$$

$$\hat{\pi}_1 - \hat{\pi}_2 = .0190$$

and

$$\sigma_{\hat{\pi}_1-\hat{\pi}_2} = \sqrt{\frac{\hat{\pi}_1(1-\hat{\pi}_1)}{n_1} + \frac{\hat{\pi}_2(1-\hat{\pi}_2)}{n_2}} = \sqrt{\frac{.0479(.9521)}{2,128} + \frac{.0289(.9711)}{1,072}} = .0069$$

Therefore

$$.0190 - 1.645(.0069) \le \pi_1 - \pi_2 \le .0190 + 1.645(.0069)$$

$$.0190 - .0114 \le \pi_1 - \pi_2 \le .0190 + .0114$$

$$.0076 \le \pi_1 - \pi_2 \le .0304$$

Note:

$n_1\hat{\pi}_1$, $n_1(1-\hat{\pi}_1)$, $n_2\hat{\pi}_2$, $n_2(1-\hat{\pi}_2)$ are all greater than 5 so use of the normal approximation should provide a good approximation.

9.25 The steps for a formal test of two proportions are given in the text.

$$H_0: \qquad \pi_1 - \pi_2 = 0$$

H_a: $\pi_1 - \pi_2 \neq 0$

T.S.:

$$z = \frac{\hat{\pi}_1 - \hat{\pi}_2 - 0}{\sigma_{\hat{\pi}_1 - \hat{\pi}_2}} = \frac{.019}{.0069} = 2.75$$

R.R.:   For $\alpha = .1$ reject H_0 if $z > 1.645$ or $z < -1.645$

Conclusion: Reject H_0

Alternatively, we could simply have observed that the confidence interval in Exercise 9.24 does not include 0.00. Therefore, reject H_0.

9.26 We note first that we want a two-tailed p-value, because our research hypothesis was two-sided. As with any p-value, find the probability of a test statistic at least as extreme as the actual. In Exercise 9.25, $z_{actual} = 2.75$.

$$p\text{-value} = P(Z > 2.75 \text{ or } Z < -2.75) = 2(.0030) = .0060$$

This value is substantially smaller than $\alpha = .10$, so once again we reject the null hypothesis and support the research hypothesis of a real difference in proportions.

9.6   Chi-Squared Tests for Count Data

9.35 a. Appendix Table 2, in the $\mu = 3.8$ column, is used to find the probability for each number of arrivals. The probabilities are reported in the column labeled "Theoretical Proportions" in the table given in the next part.

b. To calculate the expected frequencies, use the fact that

$$E_i = n\pi_i \text{ where } n = 2,000$$

The expected frequencies are reported in the table below.

The following table summarizes the information needed for the goodness of fit test desired.

Number of arrivals per minute	Theoretical Proportions π_i	Expected Frequencies $n\pi_i$	Observed Frequencies n_i	$n_i - E_i$
0	.0224	44.8	38	−6.8
1	.0850	170.0	155	−15.0
2	.1615	323.0	328	5.0
3	.2046	409.2	392	−17.2
4	.1944	388.8	415	26.2
5	.1477	295.4	399	103.6
6	.0936	187.2	170	−17.2
7	.0508	101.6	61	−40.6
8	.0241	48.2	27	−21.2
9 or more	.0159	31.8	15	−16.8
	1.0000	2,000	2,000	0

c. We wish to test the null hypothesis that a Poisson distribution model with mean $\mu = 3.8$ jobs per minute is appropriate for arrivals of jobs to a central computer.

The chi-square goodness of fit test was designed to test discrepancies from a set of specified probabilities. That's what we have here.

H_0: $\pi_i = \pi_{i,0}$ (as specified in the above table)

H_a: H_0 is not true

T.S.: $\displaystyle \chi^2 = \sum_{i=1}^{10} \frac{(n_i - E_i)^2}{E_i}$

$$= \frac{(-6.8)^2}{44.8} + \frac{(-15)^2}{170} + \frac{(5)^2}{323} + \frac{(-17.2)^2}{409.2} + \frac{(26.2)^2}{388.8} + \frac{(103.6)^2}{295.4}$$

$$+ \frac{(-17.2)^2}{187.2} + \frac{(-40.6)^2}{101.6} + \frac{(-21.2)^2}{48.2} + \frac{(-16.8)^2}{31.8}$$

$$= 77.2595$$

R.R.: For $\alpha = .01$, the χ^2 table value with 9 df (k - 1) is 21.666.

Therefore, reject H_0 if $\chi^2 > 21.67$

Conclusion: Reject H_0. The model does not seem to be a "good fit," since the calculated χ^2 value is much greater than the table value.

9.36 One way to look at the data is to compare the expected and observed frequencies of Exercise 9.35b. It appears that in the last four cells, six or more arrivals per minute, the Poisson model systematically overestimates the number of 1-minute periods which have arrivals falling in those categories. The model also overestimates the number of periods with no arrivals. The Poisson model seems to have more variability than the actual situation warrants.

Supplementary Exercises

9.44 a. The 95% confidence interval for the difference in error proportions is

$$\hat{\pi}_1 - \hat{\pi}_2 - z_{\alpha/2}\,\sigma_{\hat{\pi}_1 - \hat{\pi}_2} \le \pi_1 - \pi_2 \le \hat{\pi}_1 - \hat{\pi}_2 + z_{\alpha/2}\,\sigma_{\hat{\pi}_1 - \hat{\pi}_2}$$

where

$$\alpha = .05 \text{ so that } z_{\alpha/2} = 1.96$$

$$\hat{\pi}_1 = \frac{39}{384} = .1016 \qquad\qquad \hat{\pi}_2 = \frac{41}{475} = .0863$$

$$\hat{\pi}_1 - \hat{\pi}_2 = .0153$$

and

$$\sigma_{\hat{\pi}_1 - \hat{\pi}_2} = \sqrt{\frac{\hat{\pi}_1(1 - \hat{\pi}_1)}{n_1} + \frac{\hat{\pi}_2(1 - \hat{\pi}_2)}{n_2}} = \sqrt{\frac{.1016(.8984)}{384} + \frac{.0863(.9137)}{475}} = .0201$$

Therefore,

$$.0153 - 1.96(.0201) \le \pi_1 - \pi_2 \le .0153 + 1.96(.0201)$$

$$.0153 - .0394 \le \pi_1 - \pi_2 \le .0153 + .0394$$

$$-.0241 \le \pi_1 - \pi_2 \le .0547$$

Note:

$n_1\hat{\pi}_1$, $n_1(1 - \hat{\pi}_1)$, $n_2\hat{\pi}_2$, $n_2(1 - \hat{\pi}_2)$ are all greater than 5, so that use of the normal approximation should provide believable results.

b. The easiest way to answer this quesiton is to note that .00 is included in the 95% confidence interval. Therefore we must retain the null hypothesis, and cannot support the research hypothesis very strongly at all.

Alternatively, we can carry out a formal statistical test:

H_0: $\quad \pi_1 - \pi_2 = 0$

H_a: $\quad \pi_1 - \pi_2 \neq 0$

T.S.:

$$z = \frac{\hat{\pi}_1 - \hat{\pi}_2 - 0}{\sigma_{\hat{\pi}_1 - \hat{\pi}_2}} = \frac{.0153}{.0201} = .7612$$

R.R.: For $\alpha = .05$, reject H_0 if $z > 1.96$ or $z < -1.96$

Conclusion: Do not reject H_0. The research hypothesis that the proportions of accounts in error are different for the two banks is not supported by the data. Note that 0 is included in the confidence interval of part a.

9.45 We want a two-tailed p-value in this case. We can use the z table (Appendix Table 3). The table entry for $z = .76$ is .2764, so the one-tail area is .2236.

$$p\text{-value} = P(Z > .76 \text{ or } Z < -.76) = 2(.2236) = .4472$$

9.46 a. The 90% confidence interval for the difference in means is

$$\bar{y}_1 - \bar{y}_2 - z_{\alpha/2}\, \sigma_{\bar{Y}_1 - \bar{Y}_2} \leq \mu_1 - \mu_2 \leq \bar{y}_1 - \bar{y}_2 + z_{\alpha/2}\, \sigma_{\bar{Y}_1 - \bar{Y}_2}$$

where

$$\alpha = .10 \text{ so that } z_{\alpha/2} = 1.645$$

and

$$\bar{y}_1 - \bar{y}_2 = 60.38 - 41.27 = 19.11$$

and

$$\sigma_{\bar{Y}_1 - \bar{Y}_2} = \sqrt{\frac{\sigma_1^2}{n_1} + \frac{\sigma_2^2}{n_2}} = \sqrt{\frac{31.68^2}{39} + \frac{19.42^2}{41}} = 5.9104$$

(since both n_1 and n_2 exceed 30, s_1, s_2 can be substituted for σ_1, σ_2)

Therefore,

$$19.11 - 1.645(5.9104) \leq \mu_1 - \mu_2 \leq 19.11 + 1.645(5.9104)$$

$$19.11 - 9.7226 \leq \mu_1 - \mu_2 \leq 19.11 + 9.7226$$

$$9.3874 \leq \mu_1 - \mu_2 \leq 28.8326$$

Rounding:

$$\$9.39 \leq \mu_1 - \mu_2 \leq \$28.83$$

b. We are 90% confident that the mean error *of those accounts in error* at Bank B is at least \$9.39 larger than the mean error of those accounts in error at Bank A and at most \$28.83. The conclusion applies to the population of erroneous accounts at the banks.

c. There's a small trap in this exercise. It specifies $\alpha = .05$, so the 90% confidence interval is not directly usable. Because the interval doesn't come close to including 0, it seems quite likely that we will reject that null hypothesis. To confirm our hunch, we can carry out a formal test. With such large sample sizes, it doesn't matter whether we call the test statistic t or z. Technically, we use the t' statistic.

H_0: $\mu_1 - \mu_2 = 0$

H_a: $\mu_1 - \mu_2 \neq 0$

T.S.: $t' = \dfrac{\bar{Y}_1 - \bar{Y}_2 - 0}{\sigma_{\bar{Y}_1 - \bar{Y}_2}} = \dfrac{19.11}{5.9104} = 3.2333$

R.R.:   For $\alpha = .05$ reject H_0 if $z > 1.96$ or $z < -1.96$

Conclusion: Reject H_0 in favor of the research hypothesis that the mean errors of those accounts in error at the two banks are not equal.

9.47 Because the degrees of freedom are so large, we can use the z table.

$$p\text{-value} = P(Z > 3.23 \text{ or } Z < -3.23) \approx 2(.001) = .002$$

The research hypothesis is strongly supported since the *p*-value is smaller than all of the usual α levels.

9.59 a. If the panelists knew that one coffee was experimental, they may be subconsciously biased against it. It seems reasonable that panelists presented with an advertised brand against "Brand X" would be biased. One way to make the study blind would be to cover over the labels on the coffee cans befored the panelists arrived.

b. Veteran coffee drinkers often say that the first sip tastes the best. Certainly, time order could have an effect. At the extreme, suppose all panelists tasted the standard coffee first, and the experimental one second. If they preferred the standard coffee, is that because they like the standard coffee better or because they liked the first coffee better? We couldn't tell.

To randomize the order, each panelist might flip a coin, with heads meaning "taste the one on your left first." Many other schemes are possible.

9.60 a. Each panelist gives two rating scores, one for the coarse grind and one for the regular. The ratings are paired by panelist. Note that in recording the data, the natural method would be to have three columns—panelist, coarse-grind rating, regular-grind rating.

b. The interval does not include .00 and in fact isn't even close to that value. Therefore we can clearly reject H_0 at α = .05, and most likely reject it for much smaller α values, as well.

c. Our *t* tables don't include $n - 1 = 79$ degrees of freedom. We could interpolate between 60 and 120 df. A slightly conservative (slightly wide interval) method is to use the next lower df, 60 in this case. The tabled value for 60 df and one-tail area .005 is 2.660. The sample mean is shown as 0.900 and the sample standard deviation as 1.063. The confidence interval is

$$.900 - 2.660 \, (1.063)/\sqrt{80} \le \mu_d \le .900 + 2.660 \, (1.063)/\sqrt{80}$$

or $.584 \le \mu_d \le 1.216$. This interval does not include .00 so we would reject H_0 at α = .01 as well.

9.61 The two-tailed *p*-value is shown as 5.82E-11. The E notation says move the decimal point 11 places to the left. Thus the *p*-value should be .0000000000582. We indicated that we could reject H_0 and support the research hypothesis for α = .05 and for α = .01. The *p*-value is much smaller than either α value.

9.62 a. One important assumption for the pooled-variance t approach is that the two samples are independent. In this case, the two samples are paired, because each panelist rates both types of coffee. A key assumption for the pooled-variance t approach is clearly wrong, so we shouldn't use that method.

b. The 95% confidence interval does not include a .00 difference of means, so H_0 would be rejected at $\alpha = .05$ if we really used this test. The p-value is .0002, so again H_0 would be rejected at $\alpha = .05$ (or at $\alpha = .01$ or .001).

c. The confidence interval using this method is wider than the paired-sample interval. Apparently, pairing accounted for a major source of variability in the data and helped give us more precise inferences about the underlying population.

9.63 The signed rank p-value is shown as .000, compared to the extremely small p-value for the t test. The signed rank confidence interval is slightly wider (and slightly closer to .00) than the one based on t. The signed rank method appears slightly less conclusive. Basically, the two methods give very similar answers.

9.64 The data appear only slightly left skewed. There don't seem to be any values that look at all like outliers. For a sample size of 80, the Central Limit Theorem will certainly make the probabilities correct, and the t methods should be close to most efficient, because the data seem close to normal.

9.69 a. The Minitab 'describe' command is one of many ways to obtain the means, standard deviations, and sample sizes.

```
MTB > Describe 'Days';
SUBC>   By 'Code'.

Descriptive Statistics
```

Variable	Code	N	Mean	Median	TrMean	StDev	SEMean
Days	1	21	23.95	22.00	22.95	12.55	2.74
	2	59	27.237	27.000	26.755	3.540	0.461

b. For example, here are stem-and-leaf displays from Minitab.

```
Stem-and-leaf of Days          Code = 1          N  = 21
Leaf Unit = 1.0


     2     0 99
     5     1 033
     9     1 6679
    (5)    2 02344
     7     2 5
     6     3 3
     5     3 57
     3     4 00
     1     4
     1     5
     1     5 8


Stem-and-leaf of Days          Code = 2          N  = 59
Leaf Unit = 1.0


    14     2 33444444444444
   (37)    2 5555666666666777777777788888888999999
     8     3 00001
     3     3 9
     2     4 00
```

c. The data seem moderately right skewed, but not too far from normal. The sample standard deviations are so different that we wouldn't be willing to assume equal population variances. We'd use the t' test or, as a second choice, the rank sum test.

d. A Minitab t test is shown as an example.

```
MTB > TwoT 95.0 'Days' 'Code';
SUBC>    Alternative 0.

Twosample T for Days
Code   N      Mean     StDev    SE Mean
1      21     24.0     12.6       2.7
2      59     27.24    3.54       0.46

95% C.I. for mu 1 - mu 2: ( -9.1,  2.49)
T-Test mu 1 = mu 2 (vs not =): T= -1.18   P=0.25   DF=  21
```

The p-value is shown as 0.25. Therefore we can't support the research hypothesis very strongly at all, and must retain the null hypothesis.

9.70 a. The output from Minitab contained a 99% confidence interval. Here's the relevant part of the output.

```
MTB > TwoT 99.0 'Days' 'Code';
SUBC>    Alternative 0.

99% C.I. for mu 1 - mu 2: ( -11.2,   4.58)
```

b. The interval certainly includes .00, by a great deal. Therefore, the null hypothesis of equal means must be retained. In the previous exercise, we found that the p-value was a great deal larger than $\alpha = .01$, again indicating that H_0 must be retained. There is little or no evidence that the true means differ. However, it could be (indeed appears to be) that the variability differs between the two methods.

Chapter 10

Analysis of Variance and Designed Experiments

10.1   Testing the Equality of Several Population Means
10.2   Comparing Several Distributions by a Rank Test

10.1   a. The overall mean is not shown in the output, but we do have the means for each plan. To calculate the grand mean, we use the definition.

$$\bar{y} = \frac{\sum\limits_{i,j} y_{ij}}{n}$$

Therefore,

$$\bar{y} = \frac{8{,}835 + 9{,}301 + 8{,}472 + 8{,}591 + 9{,}542}{40} = \frac{44{,}741}{40} = 1{,}118.525$$

b. SS(Between) is shown as the SS for "`plan`" in the output, as `105530`. As a check, we can calculate the result. To calculate SS(Between), we use the definition

$$\text{SS(Between)} = \sum_i n_i(\bar{y}_i - \bar{y})^2 = \sum_i n_i\left(\frac{\sum\limits_j y_j}{n_i} - \bar{y}\right)^2$$

therefore,

$$SS(Between) = 8\left(\frac{8,835}{8} - 1,118.525\right)^2 + 8\left(\frac{9,301}{8} - 1,118.525\right)^2$$

$$+ 8\left(\frac{8,472}{8} - 1,118.525\right)^2 + 8\left(\frac{8,591}{8} - 1,118.525\right)^2$$

$$+ 8\left(\frac{9,542}{8} - 1,118.525\right)^2 = 105,529.85$$

SS(Within) is shown as the "ERROR" SS, namely 38244. To verify this calculation, square each indicated standard deviation, multiply by its df (7 for each), and sum.

c. Degrees of freedom for SS(Between) = number of groups − 1 = 5 − 1 = 4

Degrees of freedom for SS(Within) = *Overall n* − number of groups = 40 − 5 = 35

10.2 The *F* statistic is shown in the oneway portion of the output as F = 24.14. The *p*-value is shown in the same section as P = 0.000. Therefore, the *p*-value must be something less than .0005.

10.3 The assumption of independence of samples is not a problem—random assignments to plans were made from 40 workers. The assumption of normality for the distribution of each plan appears reasonable; the boxplots do not show any serious nonnormality. The assumption of equal variances for the five distributions may be a slight problem here—the sample variance of Plan A is much larger than the sample variance of Plan E. Equal sample sizes may well take care of this problem, but we should be slightly wary. However, the result is very conclusive. All in all, we don't see any problem to worry about.

10.4 The Kruskal-Wallis statistic is shown in the portion of the output labeled exactly that. It is H = 26.37. The *p*-value is shown as 0.000 (and therefore is some small number less than .0005). This test gives conclusive evidence that there is some nonrandom difference among the plans.

10.5 The conclusions of the *F* test and the Kruskal-Wallis test agree. Because the sample variances of the five plans differ somewhat, the Kruskal-Wallis test may be preferred here. But since both tests reach the same conclusion it does not matter.

10.3 Specific Comparisons Among Means

10.16 a. The confidence intervals are shown in the output in the section labeled "`Tukey's pairwise comparisons`." The output indicates that the intervals are for (column level mean) – (row level mean). The two entries in the column labeled 1 and row labeled 2 are –105.8 and –10.7. This means that the 95% confidence interval is

$$-105.8 \leq \mu_1 - \mu_2 \leq -10.7$$

Similarly, we can write out other intervals.

$$-2.2 \leq \mu_1 - \mu_3 \leq 92.9$$
$$56.1 \leq \mu_2 - \mu_3 \leq 151.2$$

and so on.

b. Look for the cases in which 0.00 is not contained in the confidence interval. The following differences are significant at the .05 level. Note that the output labels the means 1, 2, 3, 4, 5 instead of A, B, C, D, E.

$\mu_A - \mu_B$	$\mu_B - \mu_D$
$\mu_A - \mu_E$	$\mu_C - \mu_E$
$\mu_B - \mu_C$	$\mu_D - \mu_E$

10.4 Two-Factor Experiments

10.21 a. In calculating the grand mean for approval ratings, remember that the figures given represent *mean* approval ratings. (The sample sizes were large enough so that the means given can be regarded as population means.) Therefore,

$$\text{Grand Mean} = \frac{\sum\limits_{i,j} \bar{y}_{ij}}{IJ}$$

$$= (1/15)(68 + 77 + 55 + 64 + 58 + 62 + 72 + 67$$

$$+ 67 + 76 + 70 + 58 + 68 + 63)$$

$$= 67$$

The grand mean is interpreted as the average approval rating of the products given by consumers in all the regions, assuming equal numbers are in each region (which may not be true in fact), and are given each product. Loosely, it is the typical approval rating.

b. By definition, to calculate the region effects, subtract the grand mean from each row mean. The region effects are calculated below.

Region	Effect
1	$\bar{y}_{1..} - \bar{y}_{...} = (1/3)(68 + 80 + 77) - 67 = 8$
2	$\bar{y}_{2..} - \bar{y}_{...} = (1/3)(55 + 64 + 58) - 67 = -8$
3	$\bar{y}_{3..} - \bar{y}_{...} = (1/3)(62 + 72 + 67) - 67 = 0$
4	$\bar{y}_{4..} - \bar{y}_{...} = (1/3)(67 + 76 + 70) - 67 = 4$
5	$\bar{y}_{5..} - \bar{y}_{...} = (1/3)(58 + 68 + 63) - 67 = -4$

To calculate product effects, subtract the grand mean from each column mean. The product effects are calculated below.

Product	Effect
A	$\bar{y}_{.A.} - \bar{y}_{...} = (1/5)(68 + 55 + 62 + 67 + 58) - 67 = -5$
B	$\bar{y}_{.B.} - \bar{y}_{...} = (1/5)(80 + 64 + 72 + 76 + 68) - 67 = 5$
C	$\bar{y}_{.C.} - \bar{y}_{...} = (1/5)(77 + 58 + 67 + 70 + 63) - 67 = 0$

c. On the average, consumers rated Product A five points higher and Product B five points lower than the average rating of all three products over the five regions.

10.22 To calculate the table of interaction effects, construct the additive model: grand mean + row effect + column effect. The interaction effect is the cell mean minus the additive model value. For example, for region 1, product A, the additive model value is $67 + (8) + (-5) = 70$. The actual mean is 68, so the interaction is $68 - 70 = -2$. For region 1, product B, the additive model value is $67 + (8) + (5) = 80$. The cell mean is 80, so the interaction is $80 - 80 = 0$.

The complete table of interaction effects is given below.

Region	Product A	Product B	Product C
1	-2	0	2
2	1	0	-1
3	0	0	0
4	1	0	-1
5	0	0	0

10.23 Recall that a profile plot has means on the vertical axis, and the levels of one of the factors on the horizontal axis. Means corresponding to a particular value of the other factor are connected by lines. A profile plot for the means is given below; as indicated in the exercise, we have put the levels of the Product factor on the horizontal axis.

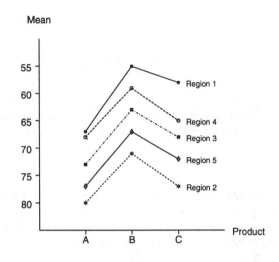

Mean

10.24 a. Yes, a small amount of interaction is present among the means. We can see this in at least three ways. First, the differences between cell means are not consistent. Product B averages 12 points higher than product A in region 1 (80 – 68), but only 9 better in region 2 (64 – 55). Second, the interaction effects calculated in Exercise 10.22 are not 0. Third, the profiles are not exactly parallel in the profile plot. The interaction is small. The inconsistency of differences is numerically small, the interaction effects are numerically small compared to the row and column effects, and the profiles are not far from parallel. since the graph by region is not parallel. Most different are the ratings in Region 1. The plots of the other four regions appear reasonably close to parallel.

b. Yes, there is one product that is consistently superior over all regions, despite the presence of interaction. Clearly, B is the favored product in every region. It gets the highest average rating of the three products, within every region. In each of the profiles, the mean rating increases as one goes from Product A to Product B, then decreases as we go to Product C.

10.5   Randomized Block Experiments

10.34 a. The system means are shown in the TUKEY (HSD) portion of the output. They are ordered from highest to lowest, so we need to make sure which is which. The means for sytems 1 through 4 are 189.83, 173.83, 211.00, and 164.33. The grand mean is the average of the system means.

$$\bar{y}_{..} = (189.83 + 173.83 + 211.00 + 164.33)/4 = 184.75$$

b. The question asks whether there is a statistically detectable difference *anywhere* among the means, as opposed to a difference between two specific means. Looking for any sort of difference is the role of the *F* test. The output shows that the *F* statistic for system is 18.41, with a *p*-value of .0000 (that is, something smaller than .00005. Therefore, the null hypothesis of equal means could be rejected at any reasonable α level, and there is a detectable difference somewhere among the means.

10.35 The output shows that there are 3 groups in which the means are not significantly different from each other. It indicates that means 1 and 2 are not significantly different from each other, nor are means 2 and 4. All other differences are statistically significant. The output says "REJECTION LEVEL 0.050," indicating that it is using α = .05.

Alternatively, the output shows "CRITICAL VALUE FOR COMPARISON 19.401." This is presumably the plus-or-minus value for Tukey confidence intervals. Any difference of means that is larger than this number is statistically significant. Checking the differences of means, we find that the only ones not larger than this value are 1 and 2, and 2 and 4. These are the same differences we declared not significant using the indicated groups.

Supplementary Exercises

10.41 a. The means and variances for each design are given below. They are shown in the output under "Average" and "Variance."

Design A	Design B	Design C
$\bar{y}_1 = 492.2$	$\bar{y}_2 = 476.5$	$\bar{y}_3 = 573.5$
$s_1^2 = 12{,}351.29$	$s_2^2 = 8{,}360.066$	$s_3^2 = 6{,}258.944$

b. The sum of square values are shown in the SS column of the output, labelled (sensibly enough) "Between Groups" and "Within Groups."

$$SS(\text{Between}) = 54{,}217.27$$
$$SS(\text{Within}) = 242{,}732.6$$

c. The df between groups is the number of groups minus one. With 3 groups (designs), there are 2 df between groups. The df within groups is the total sample size (30, in this exercise) minus the number of groups; df within groups = 30 − 3 = 27.

10.42 The F statistic is shown in the output (under "F," none too surprisingly) as 3.015. There are 2 and 27 df for this statistic. The value in Appendix Table 6 for these df and $\alpha = .05$ is $F_{.05,2,27} = 3.35$. We can't support the research hypothesis. The apparent difference in means might possibly have been the result of random variation.

The p-value is actually shown as .0658; there's no need to place bounds on it.

10.43 To carry out a rank test, the first step is to sort the data; fortunately, it already is sorted. Then rank the combined samples, lowest to highest. The ranks associated with each of the observations is given below.

Design A	Times	226	400	462	489	510	541	547	563	581	603
	Ranks	1	4	8	11	14	16	18	19	22	24
Design B	Times	329	366	409	451	465	490	517	546	577	615
	Ranks	2	3	5	7	9	12	15	17	21	26
Design C	Times	421	484	506	566	589	605	619	634	651	660
	Ranks	6	10	13	20	23	25	27	28	29	30

Then sum the ranks in each sample separately.

$$\text{Design A: Rank Sum} = \quad 137$$
$$\text{Design B: Rank Sum} = \quad 117$$
$$\underline{\text{Design C: Rank Sum} = \quad 211}$$
$$465$$

Compute the statistic and carry out the test according to the definition in the text.

Kruskal-Wallis Test

H_0:   The distributions are identical

H_a: The distributions differ in location

T.S.: $H = \dfrac{12}{n(n+1)} \displaystyle\sum_{i=1}^{I} \dfrac{T_i^2}{n_i} - 3(N+1)$

where T_i is rank sum for sample i, I = number of samples

$\qquad = \dfrac{12}{30(31)}\left(\dfrac{1}{10}\right)(137^2 + 117^2 + 211^2) - 3(31)$

$\qquad = 6.3277$

R.R.:   For $\alpha = .05$, reject H_0 if $H > \chi^2_{.05,df=I-1=2} = 5.99$

Conclusion: Reject H_0 in favor of the research hypothesis. The data indicate that the distributions have different locations.

This conclusion differs from that of the F test. For the F test the p-value is somewhat greater than .05. Here the p-value is somewhat less than .05. The most likely reason is the outliers in the data, particularly the 226 in Design A. Outliers inflate the variability within a sample and make the F test less effective.

10.44 The data sets appear to be slightly left skewed. Most crucially, 226 is an obvious outlier (as we noted in the previous exercise), casting doubt on the use of F. Note also that the sample variances are substantially unequal; but the equality of sample sizes makes this assumption much less crucial.

10.45 We need MS(Error) and the associated df, the number of means, the sample size per mean, and the appropriate α to carry out the Tukey procedure. MS(Error) was shown to be 8,990.096 with 27 df, there were 3 means based on an average of 10 observations per mean, and the α was specified as .05 (95% confidence). The desired table value is in between 3.53 (24 df) and 3.49 (30 df); conservatively, we may take the value as 3.53. The Tukey $\pm$ term is therefore

$$3.53\sqrt{8990.096/10} = 105.84$$

The means are respectively 492.2, 476.5, and 573.5. The confidence intervals are simply the differences between means, plus or minus the Tukey value 105.84.

$$(492.2 - 476.5) - 105.84 \le \mu_1 - \mu_2 \le (492.2 - 476.5) + 105.84$$

$$(492.2 - 573.5) - 105.84 \le \mu_1 - \mu_3 \le (492.2 - 573.5) + 105.84$$

$$(476.5 - 573.5) - 105.84 \le \mu_2 - \mu_3 \le (476.5 - 573.5) + 105.84$$

or

$$-90.14 \le \mu_1 - \mu_2 \le 121.54$$

$$-187.14 \le \mu_1 - \mu_3 \le 24.54$$

$$-202.84 \le \mu_2 - \mu_3 \le 8.84$$

All the confidence intervals include the possible difference 0.00. Therefore, all the intervals indicate that the difference of means may possibly be 0, and is not statistically significant. The reason is that the difference of sample means is always smaller in magnitude than the Tukey ±, so that the confidence interval must necessarily include 0.00.

10.62 a. We obtained means from Minitab, as follows.

```
MTB > name c1 'sales' c2 'color' c3 'type'
MTB > table by 'color' and 'type';
SUBC> mean of 'sales'.

 ROWS: color    COLUMNS: type

             1        2      ALL

     1   161.42   148.08   154.75
     2   150.75   119.42   135.08
   ALL   156.08   133.75   144.92

 CELL CONTENTS --
          sales:MEAN
```

b. There doesn't seem to be a huge interaction. For both colors, the mean goes down as we change from type 1 to type 2. The amount of change isn't the same, so there is some degree of interaction.

10.63 a. Again, we used Minitab, though virtually any package should be able to get an ANOVA table.

```
MTB > twoway of 'sales' by 'color' and 'type' residuals to c4
```

```
ANALYSIS OF VARIANCE   sales

SOURCE          DF        SS        MS
color            1      4641      4641
type             1      5985      5985
INTERACTION      1       972       972
ERROR           44     64297      1461
TOTAL           47     75896
```

The sum of squares for interaction is 972. Compared to the other SS, it is not large. There doesn't seem to be a major interaction.

b. Minitab did not compute F statistics for us, though many other packages will. We proceed by hand. To test for color effect,

$$F = 4641/1461 = 3.18$$

and for type effect,

$$F = 5985/1461 = 4.10$$

For both tests, we should use 1 and 44 df; because our tables don't include 44 df, we use the next lower available value, 40 df The tabled values for $\alpha = .05$ and $\alpha = .01$ are 4.08 and 7.31. Thus the type effect is barely significant at $\alpha = .05$, not at $\alpha = .01$, and the color effect is not significant at either α.

10.64 We obtained a normal plot using Minitab. The plot appears quite close to a straight line, so the residuals data appear quite close to normally distributed.

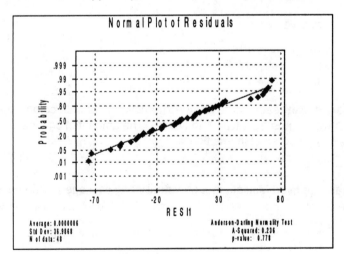

10.76 a. The value of the F statistic is shown in the output as $F = 4.26$. It has 3 and 60 df. The value in Appendix Table 6 for $\alpha = .01$ and these df is 4.13. Because the calculated F is greater than the tabled value, reject H_0. There is rather strong evidence that at least some of the population means differ. The apparent differences among sample means are unlikely to have occurred by chance.

b. Having rejected H_0 at $\alpha = .01$, we know that p-value $< .01$. The F table value for $a = .005$ is 4.73, so H_0 would be retained at $\alpha = .005$. Thus

$$.005 < p\text{-value} < .01$$

In fact, the p-value is shown in the output as $.0087$.

c. We have no indication of any bias, though it may be present. The sample sizes are equal, so the difference of sample variances shouldn't be a problem. There is no reason to suspect dependence. To check normality, we can construct stem-and-leaf displays for each sample.

```
           1                  2                  3                  4

    2 |              2 | 2            2 | 4            2 |
    2 |              2 |              2 |              2 |
    3 |              3 |              3 |              3 |
    3 | 7            3 |              3 |              3 |
    4 | 2 1 2        4 |              4 |              4 |
    4 | 9 8 8        4 |              4 | 7            4 | 9
    5 | 2 3 3        5 | 0 2          5 | 2            5 | 4
    5 | 7 8 8 6 7 5  5 | 5 6 8 7 7    5 | 7 5 6        5 | 7 8
    6 |              6 | 3 1 4        6 | 3 4 1 0 4    6 | 3 4 4 0 2 2 0 3 4 1
    6 |              6 | 5 5 5 5 6    6 | 7 6 6 5      6 | 6 5
```

Obviously there are two extreme outliers. Perhaps there is left-skewness as well, but not severely so. The outliers strongly suggest nonnormal populations. Typically, outliers make mean-type tests (such as F) conservative, if anything. Thus our rejection of H_0 is not invalidated. A test that doesn't assume normality might be even more conclusive.

10.77 a. For simultaneous confidence intervals with equal sample sizes, the Tukey approach works best. There are $t = 4$ treatments and 60 df for MS(Within). The required studentized-range (Appendex Table 7) value for $\alpha = .01$ (99% confidence) is 4.59. The form of each confidence interval is

$$\bar{y}_i - \bar{y}_{i'} \pm 4.59 \sqrt{\frac{MS(Within)}{n}}$$

$$\bar{y}_i - \bar{y}_{i'} \pm 4.59 \sqrt{\frac{74.13}{16}}$$

$$\bar{y}_i - \bar{y}_{i'} \pm 9.88$$

(The output shows a very slightly different number, 9.90 as the CRITICAL VALUE FOR COMPARISON.) Computation of mean differences gives the following confidence intervals

$$-17.06 \le \mu_1 - \mu_2 \le 2.70$$

$$-17.63 \le \mu_1 - \mu_3 \le 2.13$$

$$-20.25 \le \mu_1 - \mu_4 \le -0.49$$

$$-10.45 \le \mu_2 - \mu_3 \le 9.31$$

$$-13.07 \le \mu_2 - \mu_4 \le 6.69$$

$$-12.50 \le \mu_3 - \mu_4 \le 7.26$$

b. The 99% confidence intervals can be used to perform tests at $\alpha = .01$ rather than at $\alpha = .05$, of course. Note that only the interval for $\mu_1 - \mu_4$ excludes 0; only $\bar{y}_1$ and $\bar{y}_4$ differ detectably, at $\alpha = .01$. For $\alpha = .05$, the $\pm$ term is

$$3.74 \sqrt{\frac{74.13}{16}} = 8.05$$

The only significant difference at $\alpha = .05$ is $\bar{y}_1 - \bar{y}_4$. In this exercise, it happens not to matter to the significance results whether we use .05 or .01.

10.78 a. There are $4 - 1 = 3$ df. The required value from Appendix Table 5 is $\chi^2_{.01} = 11.34$. Because $H = 17.18 > \chi^2_{.01} = 11.34$, H_0 is rejected. Thus the p-value must be less than .01. In fact, it is shown as .0006.

b. The F test yielded a p-value betwen .005 and .01. The Kruskal-Wallis test was even more conclusive, with a p-value less than .001. We noted in part c of Exercise

10.76 that there were outliers in the data. For such data, rank tests often are more conclusive than tests (such as the ANOVA F test) based on means.

10.79 **a.** A x^2 test of independence is shown in the output.

$$x^2 = 5.67$$

There are $(3 - 1) \times (3 - 1) = 4$ df; from Appendix Table 5, $x^2_{.05} = 9.488$.

$$x^2 = 5.675 < x^2_{.05} = 9.488$$

so the relation is not statistically significant.

b. The p-value is shown as .2248. In part a, we saw that we could not reject the hypothesis of independence at $\alpha = .05$. The p-value indicates that we could not reject it at $\alpha = .10$ either.

c. We note that 3 of the 9 expected values are less than 5. With such small expected values the x^2 approximation may be a bit off. Note, though, that the x^2 statistic is not close to the table values; the approximation need not be terribly accurate in this case.

10.80 There are several ways to measure relation. We can compute rating percentages within each degree of control group. As the degree of control increases from 1 to 3, the percentage giving a "very useful" rating increases (5/16 for control 1, 6/16 for control 2, 9/16 for control 3) and the percentage giving a "not useful" rating decreases (7/16 for control 1, 3/16 for control 2, 2/16 for control 3). This fact indicates that there's a relation in the sample data. The x^2 test result says that this apparent relation could have arisen by random variation. It could also reflect an underlying relation.

10.81 The statement that there is no relation between rating and degree of control is the null hypothesis of the test. The person's statement translates as "the test proves that H_0 is true" and is incorrect. One never can prove that H_0 is true. All that can be said is that there is not enough evidence to contradict H_0. Further, the sample size is rather small, so the x^2 test will have rather weak power to detect a relation.

10.89 The output shows results for both t' and pooled-variance t. Both tests use a one-sided research hypothesis, indicated by the subcommand "Alternative - 1" and the notation "T-Test mu 1 = mu 2 (vs <)." It makes virtually no difference which one we use. The *p*-value is .006something for both tests. Therefore, we do have quite clear evidence to support the research hypothesis.

10.90 The one-tailed *p*-value for the Mann-Whitney (rank sum) test is shown as .0007. This is very clear evidence supporting the research hypothesis. The value indicates that the chances of getting at least this extreme a result, assuming the populations really are identical, is only 7 in 10,000. Because it is so unlikely to observe by chance what we in fact did observe, we reject the assumption (hypothesis) of identical populations.

10.91 There are several outliers, particularly in industry 1. The rank sum test is more efficient in the presence of outliers. The results of the tests are the same. There is strong evidence that the P/E ratio for computer services is higher, on average, than that of utilities. As expected for outlier-prone data, the rank test was even more conclusive than either *t* test.

10.92 Variability can be measured by the standard deviation. In sample 2 (computer services), the standard deviation is relatively high. Without doing some kind of formal test, we can't say that the result is more than just random variation. On the face of the sample data, it does appear that there is more variability in sample 2 than in sample 1. The boxplots also show this fact; the boxplot for industry 2 is clearly wider than the one for industry 1.

10.93 First, we need independent samples. The data aren't paired so this assumption is plausible. Second, we need to assume normal populations. In Exercise 10.91 we saw that there were outliers. The normality assumption is dubious here. This is not too crucial, because of the Central Limit Theorem. Third, we need to be sure that there was no bias in taking the samples. If the samples aren't random (and it might be hard to take random samples in this situation), there is a danger of favoring one type of company in one industry, but a different type in the other. Finally, we need independence within each sample. There may be some carryover effect from one company to another. However, we don't have information about that. From what we know, the normality assumption is fairly clearly wrong, and some of the other assumptions are doubtful.

10.102 a. Using the relevant definitions we find

$$\bar{y} = \frac{12(21.167) + 9(15.444) + 18(27.389)}{12 + 9 + 18} = 22.718$$

$$SS(\text{Between}) = 12(21.167 - 22.718)^2 + 9(15.444 - 22.718)^2 + 18(27.389 - 22.718)^2$$

$$= 897.80$$

$$SS(\text{Within}) = (12 - 1)(68.152) + (9 - 1)(53.528) + (18 - 1)(66.369)$$

$$= 2,306.17$$

The SS(Between) value differs (in the fourth digit, really) from that shown in the exercise. Presumably the indicated SS was calculated from the raw data rather than the (rounded off) summary data.

b. The null hypothesis is H_0: $\mu_B = \mu_E = \mu_{LA}$. F is shown in the output as 7.007, with a p-value of .0027. The p-value is much less than $\alpha = .05$, so that H_0 is rejected and there is a statistically significant (detectable) difference.

10.103 One of the assumptions of the F test in analysis of variance is that the populations are normal. Right-skewness in all samples strongly suggests that the populations are not normal. The Kruskal-Wallis test does not require an assumption of normal populations. Therefore, it is more appropriate in this situation.

10.104 We need a χ^2 test of the null hypothesis that managerial potential is independent of type of education.

The $\hat{E}_{ij}$ table is

	Little	Some	High
Business	5.231	3.692	3.077
Engineering	3.923	2.769	2.308
Liberal Arts	7.846	5.538	4.615

$$\chi^2 = \frac{(7 - 5.231)^2}{5.231} + \frac{(3 - 3.692)^2}{3.692} + \cdots + \frac{(7 - 4.615)^2}{4.615}$$

$$= 16.61$$

There are $(3 - 1)(3 - 1) = 4$ df. From Appendix Table 5, $\chi^2_{.05} = 9.488$. Reject H_0 because $\chi^2 > \chi^2_{.05}$

Chapter 11

Linear Regression and Correlation Methods

11.1   The Linear Regression Model
11.2   Estimating Model Parameters

11.7 a. The scatterplot could be drawn by hand. The *X* axis ranges from 60 to 120 and the *Y* axis ranges from 3.0 to 5.8. Each (*x*, *y*) pair should be one point in the plot, so that the first point would be (60, 4.6). Alternatively, we had a computer program (Execustat, in this case) plot the data, with the following result.

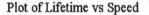

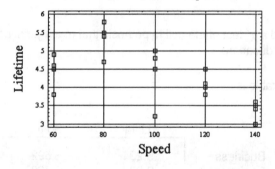

There seems to be a fair degree of relation. We can see a definite pattern of lifetimes changing as speed changes. However, it doesn't seem to be a straight-line relation. The lifetimes first increase, then decrease, as speed increases.

b. There is one point at speed = 100 that falls quite a bit below the others. It certainly seems to be an outlier. Because it occurs right at the average value of the independent variable (speed), it has very low leverage, and therefore can not have high influence.

11.8 a. The output shows the coefficients of the regression line in the Coefficient column. The intercept is 6.03 and the slope is –.017.

b. The slope has a negative sign, indicating a decreasing relation. According to the equation, as speed increases, lifetimes tend to decrease. The scatterplot indicates that this is misleading. The relation is not a straight line. The lifetimes first increase, then decrease, as speed increases.

c. The output shows this number as `Standard Error = 0.6324`. As a check, take the square root of MS(Residual), which is 0.400. The interpretation of this standard deviation uses the Empirical Rule. About 95% of all prediction errors will be smaller (in magnitude) than ± 2(.6324) = ± 1.2648.

11.9 a. The prediction equation predicts lifetime as 6.03 − .017 X, where the independent variable X is speed. To find predicted values at various speeds, simply plug those speeds into the regression equation. The predicted lifetimes for $X = 60$, 80, 100, 120, and 140 are respectively:

$$6.03 - .017(60)\ = 5.01$$
$$6.03 - .017(80)\ = 4.67$$
$$6.03 - .017(100) = 4.33$$
$$6.03 - .017(120) = 3.99$$
$$6.03 - .017(140) = 3.65$$

b. All the actual lifetimes at both speed extremes ($X = 60$ and $X = 140$) are below the predicted values. On the other hand, all the lifetimes at $X = 80$ are above the predicted value, as are all but one of the values at $X = 100$, and all but one of the values at $X = 120$. Therefore, the actual values at both extremes are lower than predicted, and most of the actual values in the middle of the data are higher than predicted. This pattern indicates that a straight-line prediction is not appropriate. If the prediction is reasonable, there shouldn't be any systematic pattern of deviations from predicted.

11.3   Inferences about Regression Parameters

11.13 a. The 90% confidence interval for β_1 is

$$\hat{\beta}_1 - t_{\alpha/2}\, s_\epsilon \sqrt{\frac{1}{S_{xx}}} \le \beta_1 \le \hat{\beta}_1 + t_{\alpha/2}\, s_\epsilon \sqrt{\frac{1}{S_{xx}}}$$

where

$\hat{\beta}_1 = .0111049$

$s_\epsilon \sqrt{\dfrac{1}{S_{xx}}}$ is the standard error of the slope, shown in the output as .0008453

$\alpha = .10$ and $df = 12 - 2 = 10$, so that $t_{\alpha/2} = 1.812$

Therefore,

$$.0111049 - (1.812)(.0008453) \leq \beta_1 \leq .0111049 + (1.812)(.0008453)$$

$$.00957 \leq \beta_1 \leq .01264$$

b. This hypothesis states that the number of independent businesses (x) in the population of zip-code areas has no effect in predicting the number of bank branches (y) in these areas.

c. One of the fundamental reasons for locating a bank branch in a particular area is to serve the small businesses located in that area. Therefore, we have good reason to presume that, if any relation exists, the number of bank branches increases with the number of businesses in the same area. Therefore H_a should be stated as:

H_a: $\beta_1 > 0$

d. The output for Exercise 11.5 shows $t = 13.138$.

H_0: $\beta_1 = 0$

H_a: $\beta_1 > 0$

T.S.: $t = 13.138$

R.R.:   At $\alpha = .05$ and $df = 10$, reject H_0 if $t > 1.812$

Conclusion: Reject H_0. The data conclusively support H_a.

11.14 The t value (13.138) shown in the output for Exercise 11.5 has a p-value of .000 in that output. The test statistic is so large that it's even much greater than the tabulated t at $\alpha = .001$ ($t_{.001} = 4.144$). The p-value of the test is very close to .0000. That is, p-value $= P(t > 13.138) \approx .0000$.

11.21 a. The regression equation using *x* is

$$\hat{y} = 14.2917 + 1.475\ x$$

Therefore, if $x_{n+1} = 20$, then

$$\hat{y}_{n+1} = 14.2917 + 1.475(20)$$

$$= 43.792$$

as shown in the "Fit" entry of the output.

b. The regression equation using x' is

$$\hat{y} = 14.8755 + 10.522\ x'$$

Therefore, if $x_{n+1} = 20$ so that $x' = \log 20 = 1.301$, then

$$\hat{y}_{n+1} = 14.8755 + 10.522(1.301)$$

$$= 28.565$$

The "Fit" entry shows a subtle error in using output. The subcommand asked to predict at a value of $x' = 20$. But this asks for prediction at a value of $\log_{10}(x)$; what we should do is ask for a value of $x' = \log_{10}(20)$. Therefore, the output is not what we really wanted.

c. The s_e of predicting *y* with x' is 1.13. This is smaller than the s_e of predicting *y* with *x* which is 1.36. Therefore, it seems that prediction with x' is more reasonable. However, note that $x = 20$ (or $x' = \log(20) = 1.301$) is much larger than any data value; extrapolation is a serious problem.

11.22 The 95% prediction interval for Y_{n+1}, using x' in prediction is

$$\hat{y}_{n+1} - t_{\alpha/2}\, s_e \sqrt{1 + \frac{1}{n} + \frac{(x_{n+1} - \bar{x}')^2}{S_{x'x'}}} \le Y_{n+1}$$

$$\le \hat{y}_{n+1} + t_{\alpha/2}\, s_{\hat{\alpha}} \sqrt{1 + \frac{1}{n} + \frac{(x_{n+1} - \bar{x}')^2}{S_{x'x'}}}$$

where

$\alpha = .05$ and df = 10 so that $t_{\alpha/2} = 2.228$

$\hat{y}_{n+1} = 28.567$

$s_e = 1.13$

$\bar{x} = .505$

$S_{xx} = 1.227$

Therefore,

$$28.567 - (2.228)(1.131) \sqrt{1 + \frac{1}{12} + \frac{(1.301 - .505)^2}{1.227}} \le Y_{n+1}$$

$$\le 28.567 + (2.228)(1.131) \sqrt{1 + \frac{1}{12} + \frac{(1.301 - .505)^2}{1.227}}$$

$$25.376 \le Y_{n+1} \le 31.753$$

11.5   Correlation

11.25   a.   The r^2_{yx} value is labelled R-Squared = 99.64% on the computer output.

$$r^2_{yx} = .9964$$

This very large value indicates that virtually all the variation in total cost is accounted for by variation in runsize. Therefore the sum of squares for Model is extremely large compared to the Error sum of squares.

b. Since β_1 is positive, there must be a positive relation between y and x and the sign of r_{yx} should be positive. The output confirms that the correlation coefficient is .998, about as positive a correlation as we can get.

c. The value of r_{yx} would be smaller than what we obtained with the full data. In general, a wide range of x values tends to increase the magnitude of r_{yx} and a small range to decrease it. Restricting the range of data to runsize less than 1.8 would tend to decrease the correlation.

Supplementary Exercises

11.33 a. The coefficients are shown in the Coef. column. The least squares regression line is

$$\text{predicted } y = 5.890659 + .0148652 \, x.$$

b. A two-sided test of this null hypothesis is given by the output and the p-value of the t test shown there. For a one-sided research hypothesis, we must first check that the sample coefficient at least goes in the hypothesized direction. In this case, it does; the sample slope is positive. For a one-tailed p-value, we now can divide the two-tailed value by two and obtain a one-tailed p-value of .0107.

11.34 a. The regression line obtained from the Coef column is

$$\text{predicted } y = 1.007445 + 2.307015 \, \ln(x).$$

b. The t statistic is shown as 7.014, with a p-value of .000; we could divide the p-value by 2, but in this case it won't matter.

11.35 The regression line using $\ln(x)$ appears to be the better fit. Comparison of the plots indicates $\ln(x)$ gives a more nearly linear fit to y than does x. Also, the residual standard deviation in Exercise 11.34 is smaller than the residual standard deviation in Exercise 11.33. (2.0135 vs. 2.3801)

11.36 a. The Stata output is convenient in that it actually gives confidence intervals for the true slope and intercept, without the necessity for any more calculation. The confidence for the slope (coefficient of Size) is shown as

$$.008291 \le \beta_1 \le .0214394$$

b. Again, we need only read the result from the output. The desired interval is

$$1.461508 \le \beta_1 \le 3.152523$$

11.37 We prefer the model using the natural logarithm. As indicated in Exercise 11.35, it fits the data better. The x values are shown in $10,000 units, so we want to predict at $x = 75$. The natural logarithm of 75 is (thanks to our calculator) 4.3175. Putting this number into the regression equation, we find that the predicted length is $1.007445 + 2.307015(4.3175) = 10.97$. A rough 95% prediction interval, neglecting extrapolation issues and t tables, simply takes the prediction $\pm$ 2 times the residual standard deviation. That standard deviation is shown as `Root MSE = 2.0135`. Therefore, our rough prediction interval is $10.97 \pm 2(2.0135)$, or between 6.94 and 15.00. This is quite a wide interval and not a very accurate prediction.

11.48 a. We obtained a plot using Systat. Other packages should give basically similar patterns.

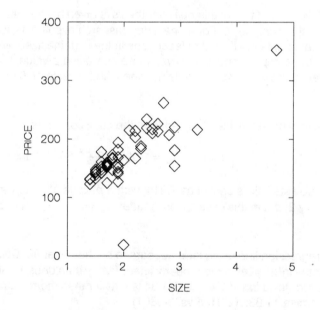

There is a general pattern for price to increase as size increases.

b. One house is shown as having a size of about 2, but a very low price. It seems to be an outlier, well below any reasonable line through the data. Because its size is near the mean size, it does not have high leverage.

120

c. Systat's MGLH program produced the following regression output for the outlier-included data.

```
DEP VAR:  PRICE    N:  57   MULTIPLE R: .767  SQUARED MULTIPLE R:   .589
ADJUSTED SQUARED MULTIPLE R: .581  STANDARD ERROR OF ESTIMATE:   29.141

VARIABLE    COEFFICIENT   STD ERROR   STD COEF TOLERANCE   T  P(2 TAIL)

CONSTANT       51.077       13.970     0.000 1.0000000  3.656   0.001
   SIZE        59.152        6.666     0.767 1.0000000  8.873   0.000


                      ANALYSIS OF VARIANCE

   SOURCE    SUM-OF-SQUARES    DF   MEAN-SQUARE    F-RATIO        P

 REGRESSION     66861.770      1     66861.770     78.733      0.000
 RESIDUAL       46707.472     55       849.227
```

The regression equation predicts price as 51.077 + 59.152 size.

d. We found the outlier (it appeared to have a decimal point in the wrong place) by using the Systat editor. After removing it, we used Systat's MGLH again to obtain the following.

```
   1 CASES DELETED DUE TO MISSING DATA.

DEP VAR:  PRICE     N:  56   MULTIPLE R: .859  SQUARED MULTIPLE R: .737
ADJUSTED SQUARED MULTIPLE R:  .733  STANDARD ERROR OF ESTIMATE:   20.958

VARIABLE    COEFFICIENT   STD ERROR   STD COEF TOLERANCE    T   P(2 TAIL)

CONSTANT       53.987       10.055     0.000 1.0000000  5.369    0.000
   SIZE        59.040        4.794     0.859 1.0000000 12.314    0.000


                      ANALYSIS OF VARIANCE

   SOURCE    SUM-OF-SQUARES    DF   MEAN-SQUARE    F-RATIO        P

 REGRESSION     66607.322      1     66607.322    151.640      0.000
 RESIDUAL       23719.231     54       439.245
```

The predicted price is now 53.987 + 59.040 size. The slope changed very little, because the outlier had very little leverage.

e. In the outlier-included model, the residual standard deviation was shown as STANDARD ERROR OF ESTIMATE 29.141. In the outlier-excluded model, the residual standard deviation is 20.958. Deleting the outlier reduced the standard deviation a great deal. Because it is based on squared error, the residual standard deviation is very sensitive to outliers.

11.49 a. The output from part d of the previous exercise included the following results.

VARIABLE	COEFFICIENT	STD ERROR	STD COEF	TOLERANCE	T	P(2 TAIL)
CONSTANT	53.987	10.055	0.000	1.0000000	5.369	0.000
SIZE	59.040	4.794	0.859	1.0000000	12.314	0.000

ANALYSIS OF VARIANCE

SOURCE	SUM-OF-SQUARES	DF	MEAN-SQUARE	F-RATIO	P
REGRESSION	66607.322	1	66607.322	151.640	0.000
RESIDUAL	23719.231	54	439.245		

The intercept term indicates that the predicted price of a house of size 0 is 53.987. A house of size 0 is obviously silly, though perhaps the value could be interpreted as the price of the land with no building. In any case, a size of 0 is well outside the range of data. Therefore, the intercept shouldn't be taken too seriously.

b. If the slope were 0, that would mean that the predicted price of large houses would be the same as the predicted price of small ones. Obviously, this isn't true in fact; large houses cost more than small ones. The t statistic for the coefficient of size is 12.314, with a p-value of 0.000. Thus H_0 can be rejected overwhelmingly.

c. The output shows a slope of 59.040 and a standard error of 4.794. The degrees of freedom for error are 54. Note that the sample size in effect was 56 and the error df = $n - 2$. Conservatively, we can go to the next lower df shown in the t table, namely 40. The entry for a one-tail area of .025 (corresponding to a two-tail area of .05 and 5% confidence) is 2.021. The confidence interval is 59.040 ± 2.021(4.794), or 49.35 ≤ slope ≤ 68.73.

11.50 a. We "tricked" Systat into giving a predicted value and standard error by giving a false price value to a case with a size of 5.0. We assigned this case a weight of 0 in computing the regression; all other cases had weight 1. The results:

PRICE	SIZE	ESTIMATE	SEPRED
388.000	5.000	349.188	14.586

Again, the price shown is false and irrelevant. The key is that the predicted value is 349.188 and the standard error for the individual prediction is 14.586. Ideally, we should use a *t* table with 54 df; once again, we use the next lowest df value that's actually in our tables, namely 40 df As in the previous exercise, that value is 2.021. Thus the prediction interval is 349.188 ± 2.021(14.586), or

$$319.71 \le Y_{n+1} \le 378.67$$

A value of 5.000 for size is far beyond our data (and you might know that a 5,000 square foot house is very large indeed). Therefore, the prediction is an unwise extrapolation.

b. The plot (excluding the outlier) obtained from Systat is shown below.

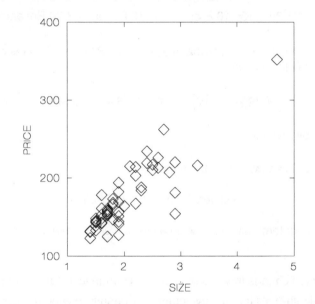

We don't think there's constant variance. Most of the data at the low end are concentrated in a relatively narrow interval. Also, recall that the numbers within the plot (for example, the 3 and 5 near the lower left corner) indicate multiple observations very near the same value. Most of these multiple observations occur at the low end of the scale. It appears that variability increases as size increases.

c. We made a prediction for a size at the high end of the scale. The assumption is that the variance is constant, but in fact the variance seems to be larger at the high end of the size scale. Thus, our prediction interval probably doesn't allow a big enough ± term.

Chapter 12

Multiple Regression Methods

12.1   The Multiple Regression Model
12.2   Estimating Multiple Regression Coefficients

12.1 a. The estimated regression equation, with results rounded to two decimal places, is

$$\hat{y} = 326.39 + 136.10 \text{ Promo} - 61.18 \text{ Devel} - 43.70 \text{ Research}$$

b. `MS(Residual)` is shown under that name as 656.811614. The residual standard deviation can be calculated as

$$\sqrt{\text{MS(Residual)}} = \sqrt{656.811614} = 25.628$$

This value is shown as `Root MSE`.

c. SS(Residual) is shown under the heading `ss`:

$$\text{SS(Residual)} = 13{,}136.2323$$

The coefficient of determination is shown as `R-square = .7697`.

12.2 $\hat{\beta}_1$ is the predicted change in y (sales), per unit change in x_1 (promotion expenses), provided that all other x's (direct development expenditures and research effort) stay constant. If we compare two quarters that differ by 1 unit ($100,000) in promotion expenses, but with equal development and research effort, then the quarter with higher promotion expenditures is predicted to have 136.0983 units ($13,609,830) higher sales.

12.11 a. The estimated model is

$$\hat{y} = 7.20439 + 1.36291 \text{ METAL} + .30588 \text{ TEMP} + .01024 \text{ WATTS}$$
$$- .00277 \text{ METXTEMP}$$

b. The results of the various t tests are summarized below. We used the t table, but we could just as well have looked directly at the p-value column of the output.

H_0	H_a	T.S. t	Conclusion
$\beta_1 = 0$	$\beta_1 \neq 0$	$t = 1.47$	At $\alpha = .05$, retain H_0
$\beta_2 = 0$	$\beta_2 \neq 0$	$t = .19$	At $\alpha = .05$, retain H_0
$\beta_3 = 0$	$\beta_3 \neq 0$	$t = 2.16$	At $\alpha = .05$, reject H_0
$\beta_4 = 0$	$\beta_4 \neq 0$	$t = -.04$	At $\alpha = .05$, retain H_0

Note: At $\alpha = .05$, df = 21, the critical value for the two-tailed rejection region is 2.079. Therefore, reject H_0 if $|t| > 2.709$.

Of the independent variables, only WATTS has been shown to have some additional predicitive value in predicting y, as the "last predictor in."

c. The output shows that the sample coefficient is -0.00277 and its standard error is 0.07722. To calculate the confidence interval, we need a t table value, one-tail area .025 (for 95% confidence) and df = 20 (the error df). This value, from Appendix Table 4, is 2.086. Therefore the desired confidence interval for the true coefficient of METXTEMP is

$$-.00277 - 2.086(0.07722) \leq \beta_4 \leq -.00277 + 2.086(.07722)$$

$$-.164 \leq \beta_4 \leq .158$$

d. The VIF (variance inflation factor) column is an indicator of the degree of collinearity among the independent variables. VIF is defined as $1/(1 - R^2)$, where R^2 refers to how well the specified *in*dependent variable is predicted by the remaining independent variables. If an independent variable is not at all collinear with the others, its VIF is 1.00. If it is highly collinear with others, its VIF value can be very large. In the output, the VIF value for WATSS is only 1.5, indicating little collinearity with the others. The VIF for METAL is 8.8, indicating fairly substantial collinearity. The VIF values for TEMP and METXTEMP are huge, indicating that each of these variables is extremely collinear with other predictors (possibly each other, possibly something else).

12.4   Testing a Subset of the Regression Coefficients

12.12 **a.** The R^2 value is labeled R-Square on the computer output:

$$R^2 = .7697$$

The F statistic (based on R^2) is

$$F = \frac{R^2/k}{(1 - R^2)/(n - (k + 1))} = \frac{.7697/3}{(1 - .7697)/(24 - 4)}$$

$$= 22.28$$

This value for F is shown in the output.

b. Testing that there is some predictive value somewhere among the independent variables is the role of the F test. We could compare the calculated F statistic to tabled values. Alternatively, simply note that the p-value for F, shown as Prob > F, is extremely small. Therefore, there is strong evidence of at least some predictive value among the independent variables.

12.13 **a.** The R^2 for the reduced model is labeled R-Square:

$$R^2 = .6978$$

The F statistic for the added predictive value of other variables is of the form

$$F = \frac{(R^2_{complete} - R^2_{reduced})/(k - g)}{(1 - R^2_{complete})/[n - (k + 1)]}$$

where

126

$R^2_{complete} = .7697$ (from Exercise 12.1)

$R^2_{reduced} = .6978$

k = # variables for complete model = 3

g = # variables for reduced model = 1

$n = 24$

Therefore,

$$F = \frac{(.7697 - .6978)/(3 - 1)}{(1 - .7697)/[24 - (3 + 1)]} = 3.12$$

b. We need to use the incremental F statistic in a formal hypothesis test. The steps follow.

H_0: $\beta_2 = \beta_3 = 0$

H_a: at least one of β_2 and β_3 is not 0

T.S.: $F = 3.12$

R.R.:   At $\alpha = .01$ with $df_1 = 2$ and $df_2 = 20$, reject H_0 if $F > 5.85$

Conclusion: Do not reject H_0. The data have not established that x_2 and x_3 have significant predictive value once x_1 is included as a predictor.

c. We just noted, in the conclusion to the incremental F test, that we can't conclude that Devel and Research add predictive value, given Promo. The apparent addition to predictive value might have arisen by random variation. It might, of course, also be an indicator of real predictive value, but that has not been established.

12.5   Forecasting Using Multiple Regression

12.18 a. The 95% limits for individual prediction in the model

$$\hat{y} = 50.0195 + 6.6436\, x_1 + 7.3145\, x_2 - 1.2314\, x_1^2 - .7724\, x_1 x_2 - 1.1755\, x_2^2$$

are located in the first part of the output under the heading `95.00% Prediction Limits`. For observation 21,

127

$$54.7081 \le Y_{n+1} \le 65.1439$$

For observation 22,

$$57.0829 \le Y_{n+1} \le 67.6529$$

b. The 95% confidence limits for individual prediction in the model

$$\hat{y} = 70.31 - 2.676\ x_1 - .8802\ x_2$$

are located on the second half of the computer output, with the same heading.

For observation 21,

$$50.028 \le Y_{n+1} \le 65.6986$$

For observation 22,

$$51.0525 \le Y_{n+1} \le 66.4345$$

c. The width of the prediction interval for Observation 21 in the first model is 65.1439 – 54.7081 = 10.4358, while the width for that observation in the second model is 65.6986 – 50.0280 = 15.6706. The corresponding widths for Observation 22 are 10.5700 and 15.3820. The interval widths for the first model are both about two-thirds those for the second model. We'd say yes, the prediction limits for the model of part a are much tighter than those for the model of part b.

Supplementary Exercises

12.19 a. The regression equation is

$$\hat{y} = -1.32 + 5.550\ EDUC + .885\ INCOME + 1.925\ POPN - 11.389\ FAMSIZE$$
$$(57.98)\quad (2.702)\qquad\quad (1.308)\qquad\qquad (1.371)\qquad\qquad (6.669)$$

Note that the standard error of each coefficient is placed below the coefficient in parenthesis, as requested. The numbers were obtained from the Coef and Stdev columns of the output.

b. The R^2 value is labeled R-Sq on the computer output:

$$R^2 = .962$$

The residual standard deviation is labeled simply s:

$$s_e = 2.686$$

c. A value that is 2.07 standard deviations away from predicted is unusual, to be sure. About 95% of all values are within 2 standard deviations of predicted, according to the Empirical Rule. However, 2.07 standard deviations is hardly a major discrepancy from 2 standard deviations. We would say this was a moderately unusual point, but hardly a serious outlier.

12.20 The conclusions of the F test and various t tests are summarized in the following table.

H_0	H_a	T.S.	Conclusion
$\beta_1 = \beta_2 = \beta_3$ $= \beta_4 = 0$	at least one $\beta_i \neq 0$	$F = 44.89$	p-value ≈ 0, reject H_0 at $\alpha = .05$
$\beta_1 = 0$	$\beta_1 \neq 0$	$t = 2.05$	p-value $= .079 > .05$, retain H_0 at $\alpha = .05$
$\beta_2 = 0$	$\beta_2 \neq 0$	$t = 0.68$	p-value $= .520 > .05$, retain H_0 at $\alpha = .05$
$\beta_3 = 0$	$\beta_3 \neq 0$	$t = 1.40$	p-value $= .203 > .05$, retain H_0 at $\alpha = .05$
$\beta_4 = 0$	$\beta_4 \neq 0$	$t = -1.71$	p-value $= .131 > .05$, retain H_0 at $\alpha = .05$

Since the F test is significant, we conclude that the independent variables, EDUC, INCOME, POPN, and FAMSIZE, collectively have at least some predictive value in predicting DEMAND. Furthermore, the t tests indicate that EDUC may have (at $\alpha = .10$) additional predictive value in predicting DEMAND as the "last predictor in"; each of the independent variables INCOME, POPN, and FAMSIZE have not yet been shown to have additional predictive value in predicting DEMAND, as "last predictor in."

12.21 a. The R^2 value for the reduced model is labeled R-sq:

$$R^2 = .942 \ (94.2\%)$$

129

b. In this case, the sequential SS in the output are not useful. The variables were not specified in the proper order, with Income and Popn added after Educ and Famsize. Therefore, we will use the outputs for the complete model (all four predictors) and reduced model (only Educ and Famsize). We will carry out the five steps of a hypothesis test. We are hypothesizing that independent variables 2 and 3 add no predictive value, given variables 1 and 4.

H_0: $\beta_2 = \beta_3 = 0$

H_a: at least one of β_2 and β_3 is not 0

T.S.: $F = \dfrac{(R^2_{complete} - R^2_{reduced})/(k - g)}{(1 - R^2_{complete})/[n - (k + 1)]}$

$$= \dfrac{(.962 - .942)/(4 - 2)}{(1 - .962)/[12 - (4 + 1)]}$$

= 1.886, when we calculate the R^2 values using the ANOVA table.

R.R.:   At $\alpha = .05$ with $df_1 = 2$ and $df_2 = 7$, reject H_0 if $F > 4.74$

Conclusion: Retain H_0

Depending on how many digits you carry, you may get a slightly different value for F. In particular, just using the values .962 and .942 shown in the output gives $F = 1.842$. The result of the test will be the same. There is little evidence that the two omitted variables add predictive value, given the other two.

12.36 a. We analyzed the data using Minitab. The correlations are shown here.

```
MTB > correlations of c1-c4

          overhead  employs    size
employs    0.426
size       0.379    0.342
personel  -0.320   -0.027   -0.140
```

None of the correlations are particularly large. The largest correlation among independent variables is between 'employs' and 'size' and is only .342. Thus, we wouldn't say that the collinearity problem is at all severe.

b. The requested plots from Minitab follow. These are "character" plots. Minitab and many other packages will also produce more elegant graphics plots. The general pattern should be similar to what is seen here, though graphics plots tend to look better.

```
MTB > plot c1 vs. c2

overhead-                        *
       -            **
       -             *
    80+    *     *    *    *              *
       -   * *
       -   *   2    *    *    *                           *
       -   2 2      *    *  *
       -   * 22  * **
    70+    2***
       -   23** *
       -  *254***
       -   2 4   *
       -  *2        *
    60+   32**
       -  *3
       -   3
       -
       +---------+---------+---------+---------+---------+------
       0       1500      3000      4500      6000      7500   employs


MTB > plot c1 vs. c3

overhead-                 *
       -                  *                           *
       -
    80+                *    *    *  * *
       -        *                        *
       -          *     *       2  *      *  *
       -        *              2       *  * *   *
       -         *    * *    2 * *    *      *
    70+       *      *  * *       *
       -      * **      * *        2    *
       -  *    *   **  *3** *    **      *        *
       -       * ***    *  *         *
       -     *        *    * *    *
    60+   *   ** *     * *     *
       -     *        *   *    *
       -       *  *    *
       -
       +---------+---------+---------+---------+---------+------
       0.0      1.0      2.0      3.0      4.0      5.0   size
```

```
MTB > plot c1 vs. c4
```

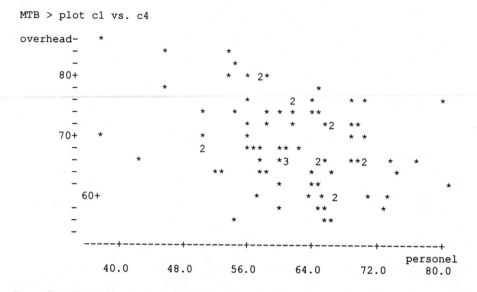

An outlier shows up clearly in the first plot, of 'overhead' against 'size'. One observation is far to the right of all the others, so it has high leverage. It appears that this point is well below any line that could reasonably be drawn through the others, so it has high influence.

c. The Minitab regression output follows.

```
MTB > regress c1 on 3 vars c2-c4

The regression equation is
overhead = 78.4 + 0.00264 employs + 1.58 size - 0.245 personel

Predictor        Coef        Stdev      t-ratio         p
Constant       78.351        5.341        14.67     0.000
employs     0.0026371    0.0007484         3.52     0.001
size           1.5763       0.6918         2.28     0.025
personel     -0.24481      0.08072        -3.03     0.003

s = 6.032      R-sq = 31.9%      R-sq(adj) = 29.4%

Analysis of Variance

SOURCE        DF           SS          MS         F         p
Regression     3      1398.47      466.16     12.81     0.000
Error         82      2983.16       36.38
Total         85      4381.63

SOURCE        DF       SEQ SS
employs        1       793.43
size           1       270.45
personel       1       334.59
```

132

```
        Unusual Observations
Obs. employs  overhead       Fit Stdev.Fit  Residual   St.Resid
 17      126    56.400    68.601     0.934   -12.201      -2.05R
 26      194    78.100    64.535     1.131    13.565       2.29R
 32     7216    76.400    86.992     4.722   -10.592      -2.82RX
 49     1866    85.600    77.209     2.296     8.391       1.50 X
 68      214    76.700    63.706     1.730    12.994       2.25R
 70     3766    80.900    79.847     2.314     1.053       0.19 X
 75      769    83.600    70.920     0.900    12.680       2.13R

R denotes an obs. with a large st. resid.
X denotes an obs. whose X value gives it large influence.
```

The equation is shown in the output as `overhead = 78.4 + 0.00264 employs + 1.58 size - 0.245 personel.` **Note that observation 32 is shown as having high leverage and a large residual.**

d. The output in part c shows that observation 32 has a large residual and also has high influence. This should be the outlier we're concerned about. To get rid of it, we used Minitab as follows (the 'wo' names stand for 'without outlier':)

```
MTB > copy columns c1-c4 to columns c11-c14;
SUBC> omit 32.
MTB > name c11 'overwo' c12 'emplwo' c13 'sizewo' c14 'perswo'
MTB > regress c11 on 3 vars in c12-c14

The regression equation is
overwo = 75.0 + 0.00516 emplwo + 1.36 sizewo - 0.205 perswo

Predictor       Coef       Stdev    t-ratio        p
Constant      75.048       5.227      14.36    0.000
emplwo      0.005160    0.001115       4.63    0.000
sizewo        1.3632      0.6653       2.05    0.044
perswo      -0.20498     0.07835      -2.62    0.011

s = 5.766      R-sq = 37.7%     R-sq(adj) = 35.4%

Analysis of Variance

SOURCE        DF          SS          MS        F        p
Regression     3     1630.78      543.59    16.35    0.000
Error         81     2693.41       33.25
Total         84     4324.19

SOURCE        DF      SEQ SS
emplwo         1     1215.98
sizewo         1      187.18
perswo         1      227.62
```

The equation including the outlier was shown in the previous answer as overhead = 78.4 + 0.00264 employs + 1.58 size - 0.245 personel. The slope of 'employs' has almost doubled, but the other slopes haven't changed a great deal.

12.37 a. The *F* statistic is shown as 16.35. It tests the null hypothesis that none of the three predictors is of any use in forecasting overhead cost. The *F* statistic is large, and the associated p-value is 0.000, so there is conclusive evidence to reject H_0. The data have shown that there is some predictive value somewhere.

b. The respective *t* statistics are 4.63, 2.05, and −2.62, with *p*-values .000, .044, and .011. All three *p*-values are reasonably small, so we have fairly conclusive evidence that each predictor adds some predictive value to the others. The evidence is most conclusive for the 'employees' variable.

12.38 Minitab has a subcommand that automatically calculates the prediction interval, as indicated.

```
MTB > Regress c11 on 3 variables in c12-c14;
SUBC> Predict at 500, 2.50, 55.

   Fit   Stdev.Fit       95% C.I.            95% P.I.
 69.763      0.787    ( 68.197, 71.329)   ( 58.180, 81.345)
```

The prediction interval for an individual value is shown as the 95% P.I., from 58.180 to 81.345. (The C.I. is for the mean rather than an individual value.) The value 88.9 falls outside the interval. Therefore, such an overhead cost would not be reasonable in this situation.

Chapter 13

Constructing a Multiple Regression Model

13.1 a. The correlation between `Crimes` and `Newcases` is shown at the very top of the output. It equals .6347.

b. The correlation between `LagCrime` and `Newcases` is shown in the second part of the output, after the package `generate` command. This correlation is .9742.

c. The "lag one" correlation is stronger. This result seems sensible; individuals convicted of *non-violent* crimes are more likely to be up for probation not immediately, but within a relatively short amount of time (next quarter). Therefore, crimes reported in any one given quarter should turn out to be a good predictor of new probation cases occurring in the following quarter.

13.2 a. The last part of the output shows a regression of `NewCases` on `LagCrime`. The regression coefficients are shown in the `Coef.` column. The equation predicts Newcases as 2.822375 + 1.73077 LagCrime.

b. The residual standard deviation is shown as `Root MSE = .21572`. This is a fairly standard name for the residual standard deviation, referring to the fact that it is the square root of MS(Error).

13.3 If we calculate "lag 10" correlations—the correlation between x_{t-10} and y_t—we would include in our computation x information from only 2 of the 12 quarters; that is,

t	x_{t-10}	y_t
11	$x_1 = 6.4$	$y_{11} = 15.1$
12	$x_2 = 5.6$	$y_{12} = 14.6$

If we were to calculate "lag 11" correlations—the correlation between x_{t-11} and y_t—we would include in our computation x information from only 1 of the 12 quarters; that is

t	x_{t-11}	y_t
12	$x_1 = 6.4$	$y_{12} = 14.6$

This is hardly enough information to obtain a correlation between crimes and new cases. With only two points, the correlation is either 1.00 or −1.00 which indicates the obvious fact that a straight line fits exactly through two points. With only one point, the correlation is undefined since the denominator of the definition is zero.

13.4   Nonlinear Regression Models (Step 2)

13.10 a. A regression analysis based on CONTRIB (as the dependent variable) and INCOME through MATCHING (as the independent variables) would be troubled by collinearity; in particular, it's likely that INCOME and SIZE are fairly highly correlated. In addition, all this regression would be doing is saying that big companies contribute more dollars than little companies. That's not too informative.

b. The variable CONTRIB/INCOME represents the proportion of pre-tax income contributed by the corporation. We introduce this variable to try to reduce some of the problems discussed above.

13.11 The idea that the effect of varying one predictor depends on the level of another is the idea of interaction. To test the suspicion that the effect of SIZE on CONTRIB/INCOME differs greatly among firms in the various industries, we could modify the regression model by introducing cross-product terms. If industry is defined by the dummy variables of Exercise 13.9 b, then the cross-product terms would be x_1(SIZE), x_2(SIZE), and x_3(SIZE). By introducing cross-product terms, we are introducing interaction into the model.

13.12 a. This exercise is describing a possible nonlinearity. If the consultant is correct, a plot of contributions divided by income against educational level would be a curve, with the slope of the curve getting steeper as education level rises. To test the suspicion that the effect of increasing EDLEVEL is itself increasing, a quadratic term, $(EDLEVEL)^2$, would be incorporated into the regression model.

b. If the consultant's suspicion is correct, the plot of residuals from a first-order regression vs. EDLEVEL would show a curved pattern. The residuals would have any straight-line part of the relation removed, leaving any curve intact. In fact, by removing the linear part of a relation, we often can see a curve more clearly.

13.5   Choosing Among Regression Models (Step 3)

13.18 a. An overall F test is used to test the hypothesis that none of the independent variables have predictive value. We have the null hypothesis

$$H_0: \qquad \beta_1 = \cdots = \beta_7 = 0$$

The research hypothesis is

$$H_a: \qquad \text{not all } \beta\text{'s} = 0$$

The test statistic is

$$\text{T.S.:} \qquad F = \frac{MS(\text{Regression})}{MS(\text{Residual})}$$

The F statistic is calculated in the output or can be found easily

$$F = \frac{MS(\text{Regression})}{MS(\text{Residual})} = \frac{.00005385}{.00003669} = 1.47$$

The p-value for this test is .208, greater than typical α values, so that H_0 can't be rejected. For this dependent variable, we don't have evidence of predictive value.

b. The output shows p-values for each t test. Only the p-value for `size` is less than even .10. Therefore, only Size among the independent variables has been shown to have statistically significant ($\alpha = .10$) predictive value as "last predictor in."

13.19 **a.** The reported R^2 in Exercise 13.18 is .213 compared to $R^2 = .069$ in this exercise. The increment is $.213 - .069 = .144$. If greater accuracy is desired, we may take R^2 = SS(Regression)/SS(Total) = .00037698/.00177115 = .21284 and R^2 = .00012167/.00177115 = .06870, respectively.

b. The required T.S. is

$$F = \frac{(R^2_{complete} - R^2_{reduced})/(K - g)}{(1 - R^2_{complete})/[n - (K + 1)]}$$

The R^2 values were computed to several decimal places in part a; k = number of variables in the complete model = 7, g = number of variables in the reduced model = 4, and n − (k + 1) = df for Error (Residual) in the complete model = 38.

$$F = \frac{(.21284 - .06870)/(7 - 4)}{(1 - .21284)/38} = 2.32$$

The F statistic is to be compared to $F_{.05,3,30\ df} = 2.92$. (We used 30 rather than 38 df as the next lower df shown in the table. Because $F < F_{.05}$, we retain H_0.

c. The C_p statistic is a means of checking whether a simpler model captures essentially all the predictive value of a more complex one. It is defined as

$$C_p = \frac{SS(Residual,\ p\ coefficients)}{MS(Residual,\ all\ coefficients)} - (n - 2p)$$

In this case, SS(Residual, p coefficients) = 0.00164949 and MS(Residual, all coefficients) = 0.00003669, from the output of the two exercises. The sample size is 46, one more than the total df. The number of coefficients p is 5, counting the intercept term.

$$C_p = \frac{.00164949}{.00003669} - (46 - 2(5)) = 8.96$$

If the simpler model captures essentially all the predictive value, we should have C_p approximately equal to $p = 5$. In fact, its value is almost 9. Therefore, using the simpler model fails to capture the full predictive value in the data.

Generally, simpler models are preferred unless more complex models are shown to be better. The C_p statistic suggests that the simpler model is not as good. The F statistic of part b indicates that the apparent difference might be chance, but again could be real. We would choose the more complex model in this case, rather than fully accepting a null hypothesis. One could make a case that neither model has proved useful.

13.6   Residuals Analysis (Step 4)
13.7   Autocorrelation (Step 4)

13.20 a. Recall that the consultant suspected that contributions as a fraction of income would be a nonlinear function of EDLEVEL. If so, there should be a clear curve in the data. We don't see any simple curve in the plot of residuals vs. EDLEVEL. Most of the points are at the left of the plot and there isn't any curve there. One might argue that there's an upward curve at the right of the plot, but that would be based on very few data points. A LOWESS smooth drawn through the data might help to see a curve, but we don't think there's much suggestion of nonlinearity.

b. To detect nonconstant variance, we look for evidence that the variability of the actual y values (or of the residuals) is increasing as predicted y increases. In other words, we are looking for a fan-shaped pattern. In the plot of residual vs. predicted (Fits1) y values, there doesn't seem to be a fan pattern. We don't see any strongly suggested nonconstant variance problem.

Supplementary Exercises

13.33 a. The SPECIALS variable is a dummy or indicator variable, representing qualitative (categorical) information. We should not code SPECIALS AS 0, 1 or 2 as indicated and use the resulting SPECIALS value in a regression. A one unit increase in SPECIALS could mean either a change from "no special packing needed" to "special packing done at station A" or a change from "special packing done at station A" to "special packing done at station B". There is no reason to assume that the two possible changes would predict the same change in any y; the coefficient of such a variable wouldn't mean much. Instead we could use two dummy variables to define special packing.

Define

$$\text{SPECIALA} = \begin{cases} 1 & \text{if special packing done at A} \\ 0 & \text{if not} \end{cases}$$

$$\text{SPECIALB} = \begin{cases} 1 & \text{if special packing done at B} \\ 0 & \text{if not} \end{cases}$$

If both SPECIALA and SPECIALB are 0, it follows by elimination that "no special packing needed."

b. From the text, we know that β_8, the coefficient of SPECIALA, is the difference in expected time between "no special packing" and "special packing at A" orders for fixed number of frequently ordered items, moderately ordered items, rarely ordered items, loose box items and for a fixed size of carton items, loose box items and fixed number of skids. Similarly, β_9, the coefficient of SPECIALB, is the difference in expected time for "no special packing" and "special packing at B" orders for fixed NUMFREQ, NUMMOD, NUMRARE, NUMLOOSE, AVSZCAR, AVSZLB and SKIDS.

The interpretations assigned to the β's for the dummy variables SPECIALA and SPECIALB can be seen by examining the corresponding expectations $E(Y)$.

For no special packing (SPECIALA = SPECIALB = 0):

$E(Y) = \beta_0 + \beta_1(\text{NUMFREQ}) + \beta_2(\text{NUMMOD}) + \beta_3(\text{NUMRARE}) + \beta_4(\text{NUMLOOSE})$

$\qquad + \beta_5(\text{AVSZCAR}) + \beta_6(\text{AVSZLB}) + \beta_7(\text{SKIDS})$

For special packing at A (SPECIALA = 1, SPECIALB = 0):

$E(Y) = \beta_0 + \beta_1(\text{NUMFREQ}) + \beta_2(\text{NUMMOD}) + \beta_3(\text{NUMRARE}) + \beta_4(\text{NUMLOOSE})$

$\qquad + \beta_5(\text{AVSZCAR}) + \beta_6(\text{AVSZLB}) + \beta_7(\text{SKIDS}) + \beta_8$

For special packing at B (SPECIALA = 0, SPECIALB = 1):

$\qquad E(Y) = \beta_0 + \beta_1(\text{NUMFREQ}) + \beta_2(\text{NUMMOD}) + \beta_3(\text{NUMRARE}) +$
$\beta_4(\text{NUMLOOSE})$

$\qquad + \beta_5(\text{AVSZCAR}) + \beta_6(\text{AVSZLB}) + \beta_7(\text{SKIDS}) + \beta_9$

c. The independent variables, NUMFREQ, NUMMOD, NUMRARE, and NUMLOOSE might be transformed because the supervisor expected travel time not to be directly proportional to the number of items because a worker could combine items found in the same general area of the warehouse.

d. Interaction means that the effect on the dependent variable of a change in one independent variable depends on the value of another variable. It is a combination effect. The supervisor expected assembly-station time to depend on a combination of NUM and AVSZ. Therefore, interaction terms (using the NUM and AVSZ variables) might be useful.

13.34 a. From the plot of residual vs. predicted order filling times, we see one very obvious outlier located at the upper left corner of the graph.

b. Nonconstant variance does not appear to be a problem. The plot of residual vs. predicted order filling times shows no evidence that the variability of the residuals is increasing as predicted y increases. There is no particular fan shape to the residuals.

c. Autocorrelation is defined as dependence of the error terms and is largely restricted to time-series data—where the data points are measured at successive time periods. The nature of this case study does not particularly lend itself to a time-series problem and therefore we would not expect to find a problem of autocorrelation.

13.35 A good transformation should allow for better prediction, as measured by either a smaller standard deviation or a larger R^2 value. Both the standard deviation and R^2 values point to "square roots" as the transformation that is more effective.

13.36 a. The R-squared value for all predictors is shown in the output as .9612. The value for the model excluding the last predictor is .9488. Therefore, adding the last predictor has increased R^2 by an increment of .9612-.9488 = .0124.

b. The following F test, based on the indicated R^2 values, is used to test the null hypothesis that the last two variables have no incremental predictive value.

H_0: $\beta_4 = \beta_5 = 0$

H_a: at least one of β_4 and β_5 is not 0

$$\text{T.S.: } F = \frac{(R^2_{complete} - R^2_{reduced})/(k - g)}{(1 - R^2_{complete})/[n - (k + 1)]}$$

$$= \frac{(.9612 - .9244)/(5 - 3)}{(1 - .9612)/[49 - (5 + 1)]}$$

$$= 20.39$$

R.R.: At $\alpha = .05$, reject H_0 if $F \geq F_{\alpha, df_1, df_2} = F_{.05, 2, 43} \approx 3.23$

Conclusion: Reject H_0 and conclude that the last 2 variables do have some incremental predictive value.

13.37 a. The regression model is

$$\hat{y} = .02436 + 1.8013(\text{SQTNFPER}) + 1.6311(\text{SQTNMPER})$$

$$+ 2.7348(\text{SQTNRPER}) + 1.1491(\text{NUMLPER})$$

$$+ .3600(\text{ASZCRPER}) + .2104(\text{ASZLBPER})$$

$$+ 1.8752(\text{SPECAPER}) + 2.925(\text{SPECBPER})$$

$$+ 1.2882(\text{SKIDSPER})$$

The residual standard deviation is .04922 (labeled s on the printout).

b. All but possibly one of the residual plots indicate no violations of assumptions. The plot of residuals vs. predicted values (FITS) does not indicate nonconstant variance; there's no evident fan shape. The plots of residuals vs. predictors don't show any obvious curves, so there's no strong indication of nonlinearity. As far as we can tell, the data aren't a time series, so there is no reason to worry about autocorrelation. The residual vs. aszcrper plot reveals one point with very high leverage (far from the others in the x direction). It may have high influence twisting the line.

13.38 a. We got out a calculator that found standard deviations. The standard deviation of the regression prediction errors is .08848. The standard deviation of the superintendent's prediction errors is .15273.

b. The standard deviation shown in Exercise 13.37 was .04922. The regression standard deviation was increased to .08848 as calculated in part a. That's not quite double.

c. Yes, the result of this study suggests that the regression model will yield better forecasts than the superintendent's forecasts; comparison of the standard deviations calculated in part a, indicate more predictive error in the superintendent's forecasts. The average error is small in both cases, 0.0128 for the regression model and 0.0421 for the superintendent's forecast. The regression model should yield smaller errors and a lower standard deviation.

13.39 a. Day number is not really a quantitative variable. Notice that day is stated as a code, with 1 standing for Sunday, up to 7 standing for Saturday. Typically, variables that have a code shouldn't be regarded as quantitative variables. Departure time is a quantitative variable, but there is no reason to expect that demand has a linear relation to departure time. Rather than a straight-line relation of demand to departure time, it's much more plausible to expect demand to peak at certain hours of the day.

b. We used Minitab to perform the regression analysis.

```
The regression equation is
demand = - 4.04 + 17.7 peakdum + 0.523 share + 4.18 income

Predictor      Coef       Stdev      t-ratio       p        VIF
Constant      -4.042      3.551       -1.14      0.256
peakdum       17.7398     0.9018      19.67      0.000      1.0
share         0.52327     0.02516     20.80      0.000      1.0
income        4.1803      0.2931      14.26      0.000      1.0

s = 5.757      R-sq = 77.0%      R-sq(adj) = 76.8%

Analysis of Variance

SOURCE          DF          SS          MS        F          p
Regression      3         35522       11841     357.32     0.000
Error          320        10604        33
Total          323        46126

SOURCE          DF        SEQ SS
peakdum         1         11781
share           1         16999
income          1          6742
```

c. The Minitab procedure to create the product terms and obtain a multiple regression model is shown here.

```
MTB > let c7=c4*c5
MTB > let c8=c4*c6
MTB > name c7 'pk*share' c8 'pk*inc'
MTB > regress c1 on 5 variables in c4-c8

The regression equation is
  demand = 1.31 - 20.0 peakdum + 0.514 share + 3.76 income
              + 0.0498 pk*share + 3.04 pk*inc

Predictor        Coef        Stdev      t-ratio         p
Constant        1.305        3.750         0.35      0.728
peakdum       -20.031        9.949        -2.01      0.045
share         0.51412      0.02648        19.41      0.000
income         3.7598       0.3090        12.17      0.000
pk*share      0.04982      0.07298         0.68      0.495
pk*inc         3.0439       0.8426         3.61      0.000

s = 5.644       R-sq = 78.0%      R-sq(adj) = 77.7%

Analysis of Variance

SOURCE       DF          SS          MS          F          p
Regression    5      35995.5      7199.1      225.99      0.000
Error       318      10130.3        31.9
Total       323      46125.9

SOURCE       DF       SEQ SS
peakdum       1      11781.2
share         1      16998.6
income        1       6742.1
pk*share      1         57.9
pk*inc        1        415.7
```

d. The R^2 value for this model is shown as .780 (78.0%). In the previous model, the R^2 value was .770. Alternatively, we may calculate R^2 as SS(Regression)/SS(Total). For this model, it is 35995.5/46125.9 = .780375; for the previous model, it is 35522/46126 = .770108. To test the statistical significance of adding two new predictors, we use the incremental F test based on R^2. Note that the complete model uses 5 predictors and has 318 error df; the reduced model uses 3 predictors.

$$F = \frac{(0.780375 - 0.770108)/(5 - 3)}{(1 - 0.780375)/318} = 7.43$$

Note: If we had used the rounded-off values .780 and .770 for the two R^2 values, we would have obtained $F = 7.22$. For 2 and 240 df (240 as the next lower df value from 318 that can be found in our F tables), the computed F statistic exceeds the table value, even for $\alpha = .001$ (7.11). Therefore, we must reject H_0: no interaction. There is conclusive evidence that there is some interaction. Note however, that the interaction terms don't improve the predictive value an enormous amount, improving R^2 by only about .01. This is a classic example of the difference between statistical significance and practical importance. We have a small, but statistically detectable, interaction effect.

13.40 **a.** We used Minitab to plot resiuals against predicted values, yielding the following plot.

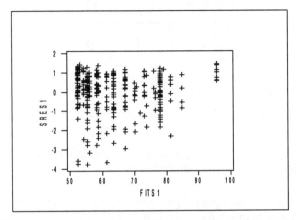

There is no evidence that the variation around the prediction equation increases as the predicted value (FITS1) increases. If anything, the plot seems to get narrower as the predicted value increases. It looks like the range of the data gets smaller as the predicted value gets bigger. That apparent change shouldn't be taken too seriously. At the left edge of the plot there are many multiple observations close to .0 residuals; these points overlap in the plot. These values will tend to decrease the standard deviation, balancing the occasional wide values. Thus we suspect that the standard deviation around the prediction equation is roughly constant.

b. Minitab plots of residuals against the predictors are shown here.

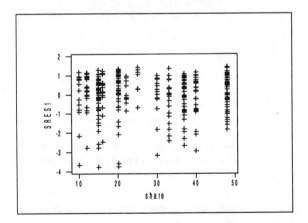

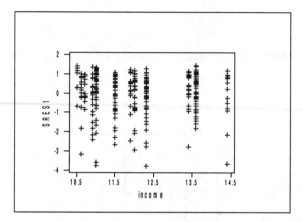

We don't see any evidence of a pronounced curve in either plot. Therefore, we see no real evidence of a need for non-linear terms.

c. The plot of residuals against the peak dummy variable consists of two stripes, one at the 0 value of the dummy, the other at the 1 value. We couldn't possibly see a curve in such a plot, so there is nothing much to be seen.

13.41 a. Minitab's `time series plot` gives a plot of the residuals in time order.

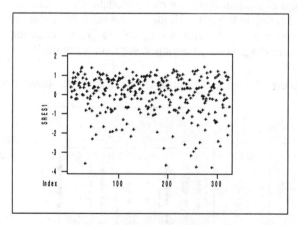

We don't see any large, obvious cycles in the data, certainly nothing that extends over dozens of flights. Therefore, we can't see any autocorrelation problem.

b. The Minitab `dw` subcommand causes calculation of the Durbin-Watson statistic. Here's some highly selected output.

```
Durbin-Watson statistic = 2.07
```

Because the Durbin-Watson statistic is very near its ideal value, 2.00, we have no evidence that there's an autocorrelation problem.

Review Exercises—Chapters 11–13

13.55 a. The regression equation is shown following (reasonably enough) The regression equation is in the output. The coefficients are also shown (to more decimal places) in the column headed Coef.

purch = −.744 + .0329 age + .00900 income + .115 owner + .00818 educn

b. The AGE coefficient means that for specified values of INCOME, OWNER, and EDUCN, each one-year increase in age predicts a .0329 unit increase in purchases. Similarly, for given values of AGE, OWNER, and EDUCN, a one-unit increase in INCOME predicts a .008999 unit increase in purchases. For specified AGE, INCOME, and EDUCN, the predicted difference in purchases between a homeowner (OWNER = 1) and a renter (OWNER = 0) is .115. Finally, for given AGE, INCOME, and OWNER status, a one-unit difference in EDUCN predicts a .00818 unit difference in purchases.

c. The intercept is the predicted purchases of a cardholder with all X's equal 0. It seems abundantly safe to assume that there are no 0 year olds with 0 income and 0 education (and 0 ownership) among the cardholders! The intercept is a prediction under absurd conditions and therefore means nothing.

13.56 a. H_0: $\beta_1 = \cdots = \beta_4 = 0$ would mean that none of the independent variables had any (linear) predictive value whatsoever in the population of cardholders.

b. The output shows

$$F = 673.85$$

with a p-value less than .0005. Computed F is vastly larger than any tabled F_α with 4 and 155 df. Reject H_0 conclusively.

c. If we choose to run two-tailed tests, relevant tabled t_α values are about 1.66 ($\alpha = .10$), 1.98 ($\alpha = .05$), and 2.61 ($\alpha = .01$). Comparing the computed t-ratio statistics, we see that the p-value for the AGE coefficient is (much) less than .01, the p-values for OWNER and EDUCN are between .01 and .05, and the p-value for

INCOME is between .05 and .10. There is strong evidence that AGE adds predictive value given the other variables, moderate evidence that OWNER and EDUCN add value, and weak evidence that INCOME adds predictive value.

13.57 Collinearity is correlation among independent variables. Looking at the table of correlations, we see that the correlation between AGE and INCOME is high at .837. In addition OWNER and INCOME have a moderate correlation of .686. The other correlations aren't as severe.

13.58 a. The largest correlation of an independent variable with PURCH is AGE, followed in order by INCOME, OWNER, and EDUCN. The order for stepwise regression is different. AGE enters first, followed by OWNER, then EDUCN, and last INCOME.

b. Basically, the coefficients of a particular variable stay fairly similar over the steps of the regression analysis. This is somewhat surprising, because the independent variables are collinear.

c. The standard deviation gets about as small as it's going to get after the first two independent variables are included, and the R^2 gets about as high as it's going to get at the same point. Therefore, we'd tend to use only AGE and OWNER as predictors.

d. The C_p statistic is a means of checking whether a simpler model captures essentially all the predictive value of a more complex one. It is defined as

$$C_p = \frac{SS(Residual,\ p\ coefficients)}{MS(Residual,\ all\ coefficients)} - (n - 2p)$$

In this case, p is the number of coefficients in the candidate model, namely 3 (two slopes and an intercept). SS(Residual, p coefficients) is not given directly from the output. It can be calculated by recognizing that MS(Residual) is the residual standard deviation squared, that n must be 160 (one more than the total df), and that the residual degrees of freedom are $160 - (2 + 1) = 157$. Therefore SS(Residual) = (df)MS(Residual) = $157(.0947)^2 = 1.40799$. Similarly, MS(Residual) for the all-predictors model is $(.0926)^2 = .008575$. Therefore, after some cleverness, we find that

$$C_p = \frac{1.40799}{0.008575} - (160 - 2(3)) = 10.20.$$

If the model has captured all the predictive value there is to be had, C_p will be approximately equal to p. In this case, it is larger. Surprisingly, it says that the two-predictor model isn't as good as the all-predictors model.

13.59 a. Recall that x_3 = OWNER is a dummy variable for home ownership. The product terms allow for the possibility of one sort of interaction. They allow the slopes of AGE, INCOME, and EDUCN for predicting PURCH to depend on the value of OWNER.

b. To test that 3 β coefficients are 0 we need R^2 for complete and reduced models. For the complete model (including the product terms) $R^2 = .947$; for this model, note that $n - (k + 1) = df_{Error} = 152$. For the reduced model (without product terms) $R^2 = .946$. The difference between the R^2 values is .001. To avoid gross roundoff error we compute

$$R^2_{reduced} = 23.1295/24.4596 = .94562$$

$$R^2_{complete} = 23.1682/24.4596 = .94720$$

We have k = 7 variables in the complete model and g = 4 variables in the reduced model.

$$F = \frac{(R^2_{complete} - R^2_{reduced})/(k - g)}{(1 - R^2_{complete})/[n - (k + 1)]}$$

$$= \frac{(.94720 - .94562)/(7 - 4)}{(1 - .94720)/152} = 1.52$$

(Using the 3-decimal place R^2 numbers in the printout gives $F = .96$.) There are 3 and 152 df; at $\alpha = .10$, F_α is somewhere between 2.13 (3 and 120 df) and 2.10 (3 and 240 df), perhaps 2.12. Because $F < F_\alpha$, we would retain H_0 even at $\alpha = .10$. Only if we were to use a very unreasonable $\alpha = .25$ could we reject H_0.

13.60 There appears to be a generally increasing amount of residual variability as the predicted values (labelled FITS1) increase. One way to see this is to note that there is white space in the upper left and lower left parts of the plot. It appears that the constant variance assumption is wrong.

13.61 a. In the original model, the output showed $R^2 = .946$ and the residual standard deviation $s_e = .09263$. The new model has a slightly higher R^2 and a slightly lower residual standard deviation. The predictive value of the new model is slightly better.

b. The only difference between the new model is the substitution of LOGINC for INCOME. Therefore LOGINC has better incremental predictive value than INCOME.

c. Yes; the *t* ratio for LOGINC is 4.02 as compared to *t* = 1.77 for INCOME in the original model. Note that in this model, OWNER no longer seems to be adding predictive value.

13.80 a. One way to test the coefficient of PROMO is to note that *t* = 8.33, far beyond *t* table values with 22 df. Another way is to note that the *p*-value for *t* is shown as .0000. Yet another is to look at the *F* statistic, 69.31, also with a *p*-value of .0000. However we choose to look at the output, the result is statistically significant at any reasonable α value.

b. The variability in SALES accounted for by PROMO is $R^2_{SALES \cdot PROMO}$, by definition. It is shown as 75.9%; R^2 = .7591.

13.81 The d statistic is 0.4331, way below the ideal 2.00 and the "trouble indicator" 1.50, indicating that autocorrelation is present. The major consequences of autocorrelation are that R^2 is biased upward and *s* and the standard error are biased downward (so that *t* and *F* are biased upward). Thus, we should view the apparent values skeptically.

13.82 a. The *t* statistic for DPROMO is 18.16, far beyond the *t* table values with 21 df. Alternatively, the *p*-value for the *t* test is 0.0000, as is the *p*-value for the *F* test. There is detectable (significant) predictive value.

b. As in Exercise 13.80, part b, we need R^2. It is shown as R^2 = .9401, so that DPROMO accounts for 94.01% of the variability in DSALES.

c. We noted in Exercise 13.81 that R^2 was likely to be too high and that the standard errors were likely to be too small (which would make the *t* statistic too large). Surprisingly, R^2 and *t* are actually larger in the differenced data. A note of caution: R^2 for the original data measures how well the original scores are predicted and isn't directly comparable to the R^2 that measures how well the differences are predicted.

13.83 In Exercise 13.81, we found that autocorrelation was present. The output in Exercise 13.82 shows a Durbin-Watson statistic of 1.4314. This is closer to the ideal 2.00 than the previous d = .43, but it is still below the "trouble indicator" 1.50. Therefore, autocorrelation seems to have been reduced, but it doesn't appear to have been entirely eliminated.